EDINBURGH

ESTATE PUBLICATIONS
Bridewell House,
Tenterden, Kent.
Tel. 05806 4225

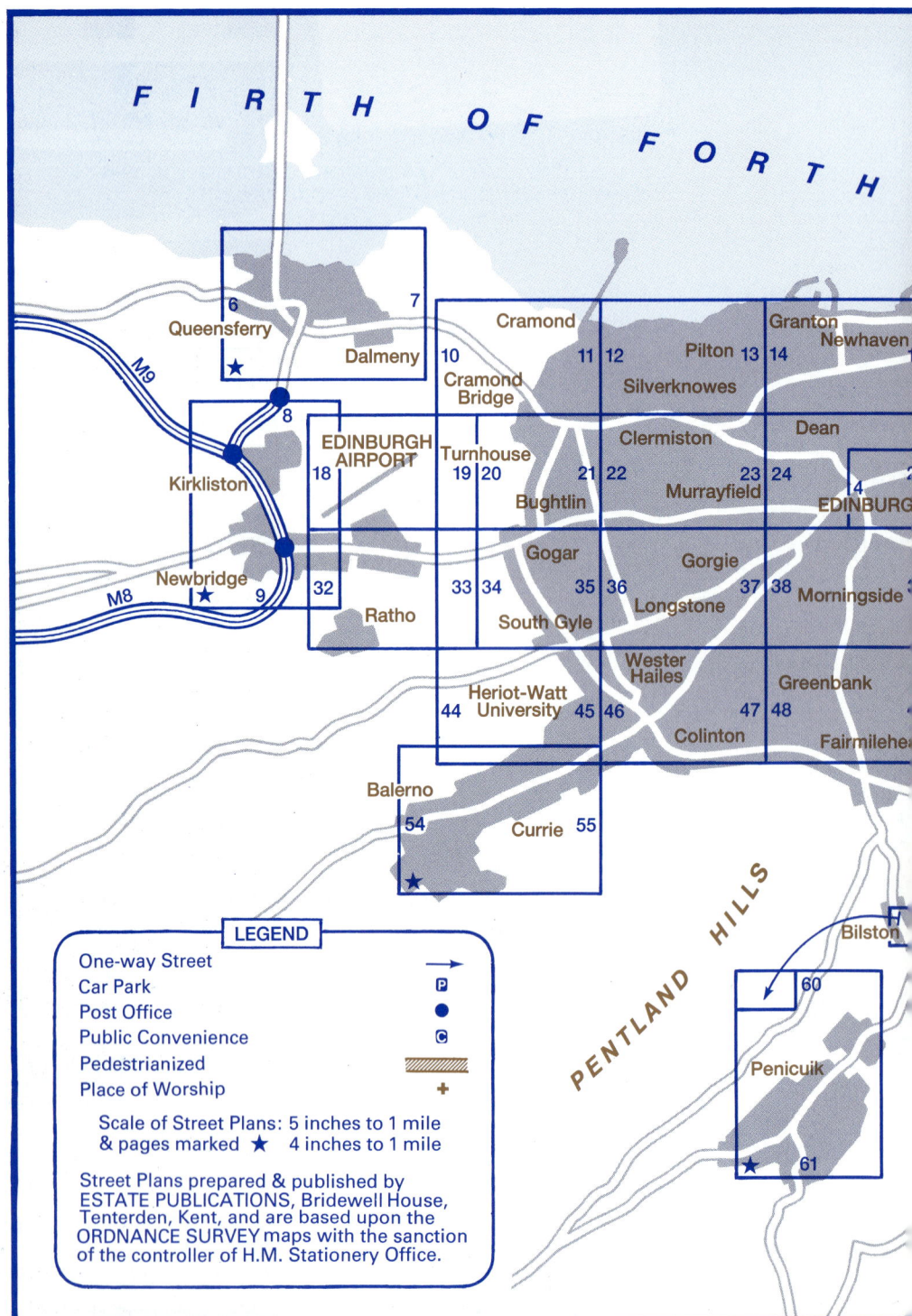

FIRTH OF FORTH

6		7		
Queensferry	Dalmeny	Cramond	Granton Newhaven	

M9

| 10 | 11 | 12 | Pilton | 13 | 14 |
| Cramond Bridge | | Silverknowes | | | |

Kirkliston

EDINBURGH AIRPORT	Turnhouse	Clermiston	Dean
18	19	20	21	22	Murrayfield	23	24
	Bughtlin			4 EDINBURGH

Newbridge

M8

| 32 | 33 | 34 | Gogar | 35 | 36 | Gorgie | 37 | 38 |
| Ratho | | South Gyle | | Longstone | | Morningside |

	Wester Hailes	Greenbank
44	Heriot-Watt University	45	46	47	48
Balerno		Colinton	Fairmilehe

| 54 | 55 |
| | Currie |

PENTLAND HILLS

Bilston

| 60 |
| Penicuik |
| 61 |

E S T A T E　　P U B L I C A T I O N S
EDINBURGH

QUEENSFERRY · KIRKLISTON · PENICUIK · DALKEITH
NEWTONGRANGE · TRANENT · COCKENZIE

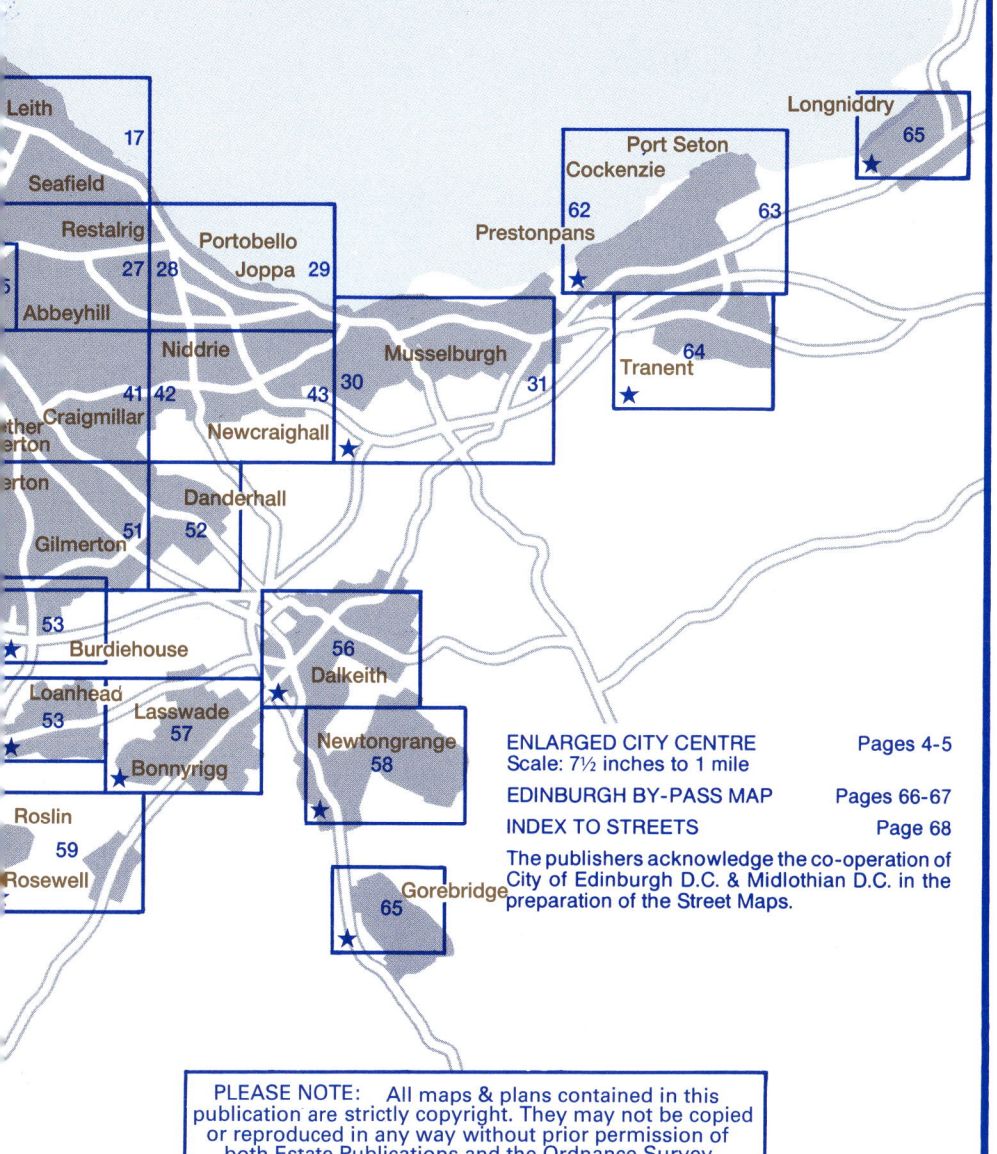

Leith 17
Seafield
Restalrig
27 28
Abbeyhill
Portobello
Joppa 29
Niddrie
41 42 43
Craigmillar
erton
erton
Newcraighall 30
Danderhall
Gilmerton 51 52
53
Burdiehouse
Loanhead
53
Lasswade 57
Bonnyrigg
Roslin
59
Rosewell

Longniddry 65
Port Seton 62
Cockenzie
Prestonpans 63
Musselburgh 31
Tranent 64

56
Dalkeith
Newtongrange 58
Gorebridge
65

ENLARGED CITY CENTRE   Pages 4-5
Scale: 7½ inches to 1 mile

EDINBURGH BY-PASS MAP   Pages 66-67

INDEX TO STREETS   Page 68

The publishers acknowledge the co-operation of
City of Edinburgh D.C. & Midlothian D.C. in the
preparation of the Street Maps.

Estate Publications 239A   SBN 0 86084 359 9   Crown Copyright reserved

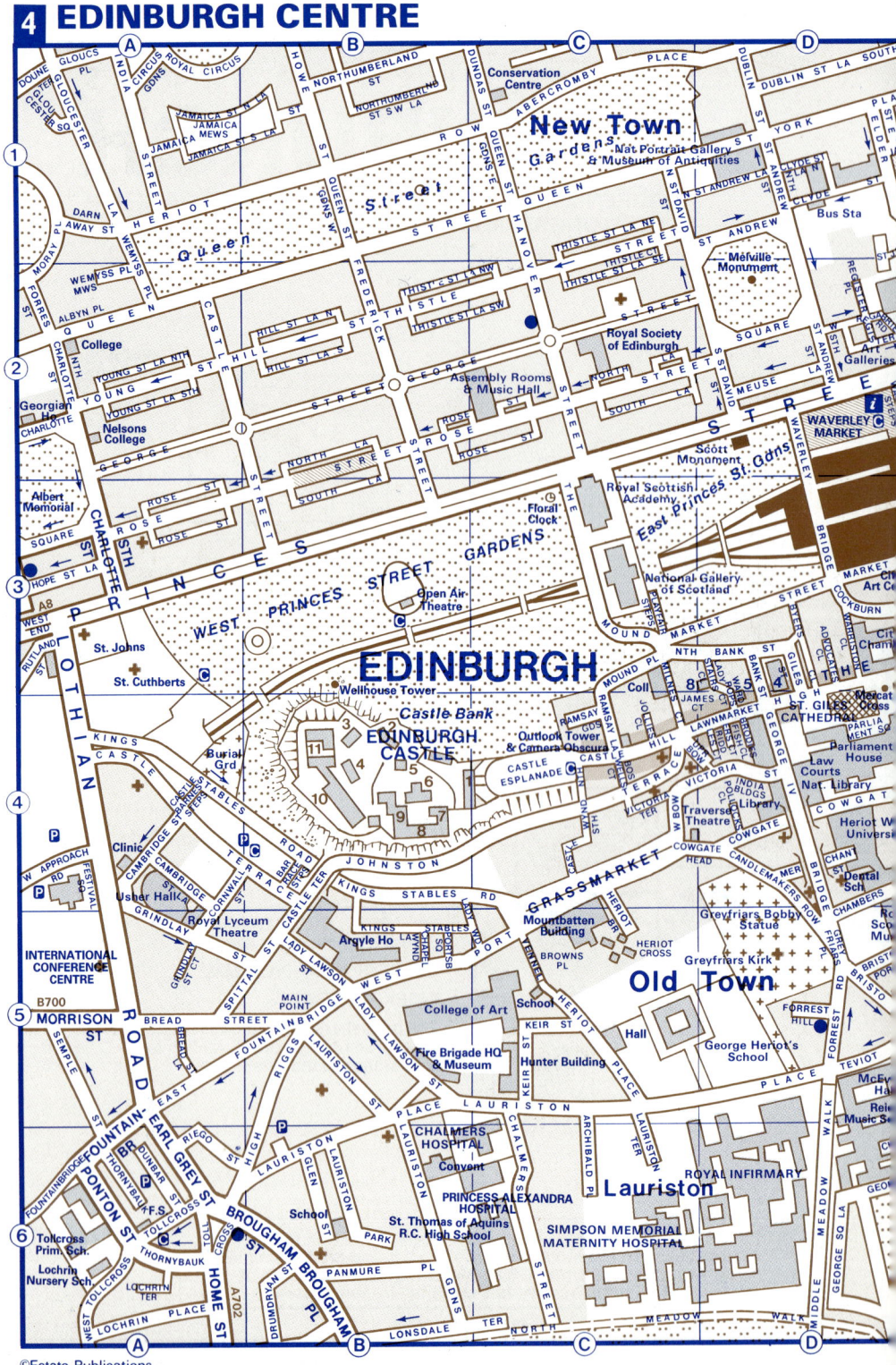

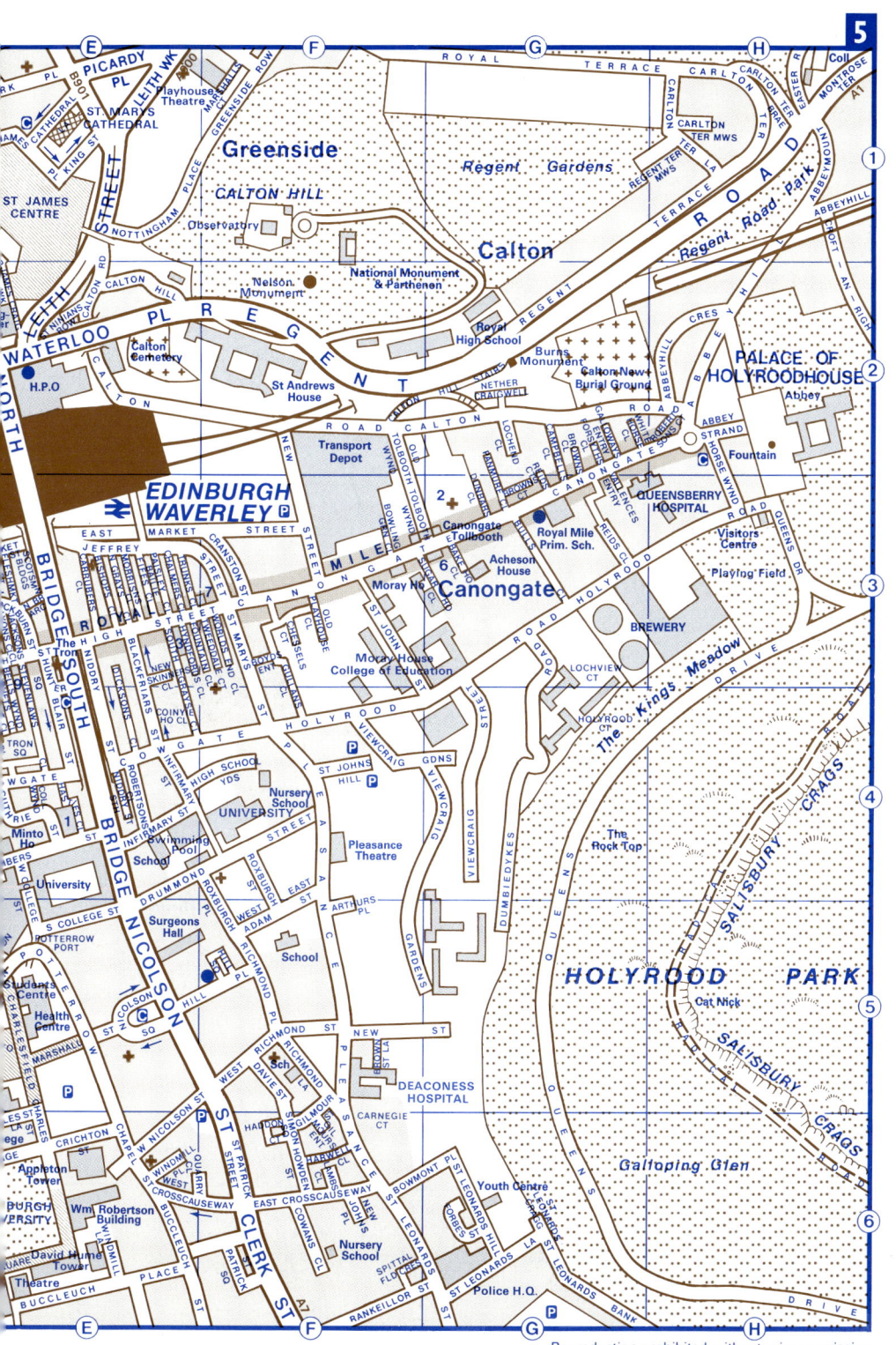

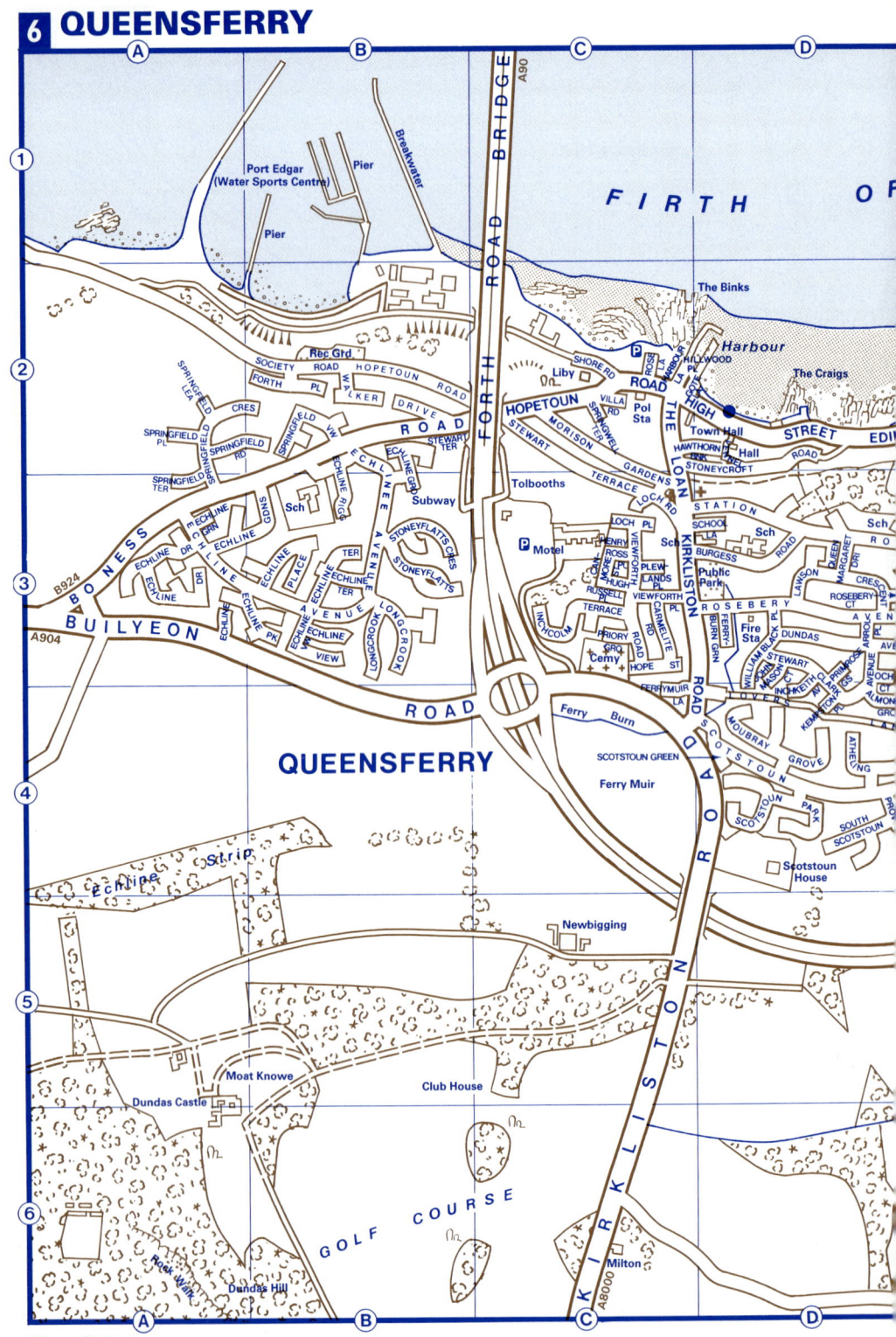

QUEENSFERRY

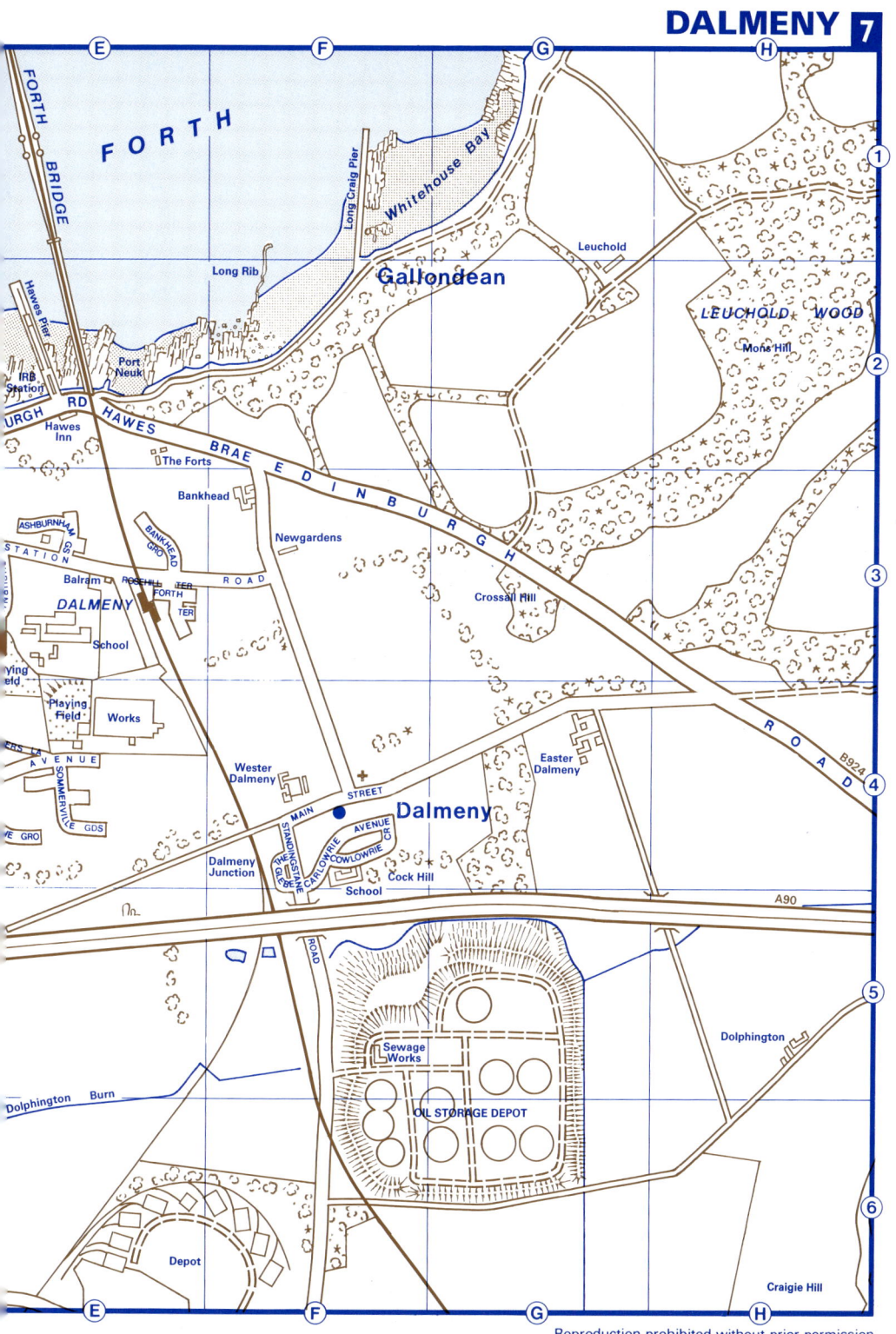

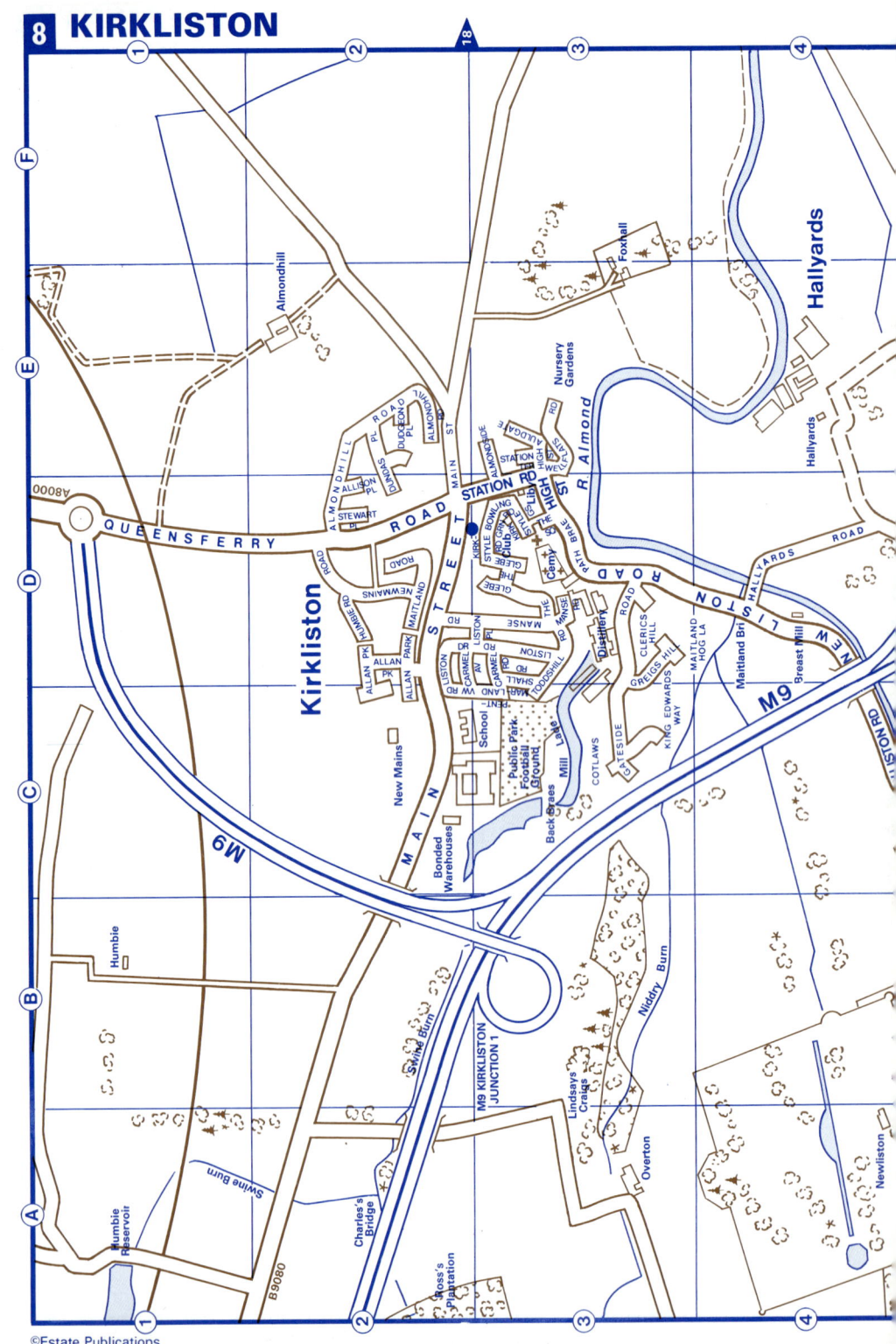

Kirkliston

Hallyards

Almondhill

Foxhall

Nursery Gardens

QUEENSFERRY

ROAD

A8000

STREET

MAIN

New Mains

Humbie

Humbie Reservoir

Swine Burn

Swine Burn

B9080

Charles's Bridge

Ross's Plantation

M9 KIRKLISTON JUNCTION 1

M9

Bonded Warehouses

Public Park Football Ground

Back Braes

School

Mill Lane

COTLAWS

GATESIDE

Niddry Burn

Lindsays Craigs

Overton

Newliston

MANSE

Distillery

CLERICS HILL

GREIGS HILL

KING EDWARDS WAY

MAITLAND HOG LA

Maitland Bri

Breast Mill

NEW LISTON ROAD

HALLYARDS ROAD

ROAD

LISTON RD

M9

R Almond

STATION RD

HIGH ST

ALLAN PK

ALLAN PARK

ALMONDHILL PL

DUDGEON PL

DUNDAS PL

ALLISON PL

STEWART

ALMONDVALE

MAITLAND

MEWMAINS

HUMBIE RD

LISTON RD

MAIN ST

STATION

STYLE BOWLING CLUB

CARMEL

CARMEL

THE MANSE

GLEBE RD

SHALL

PATH BRAE

THE WELL

Hallyards

Almondhill

©Estate Publications

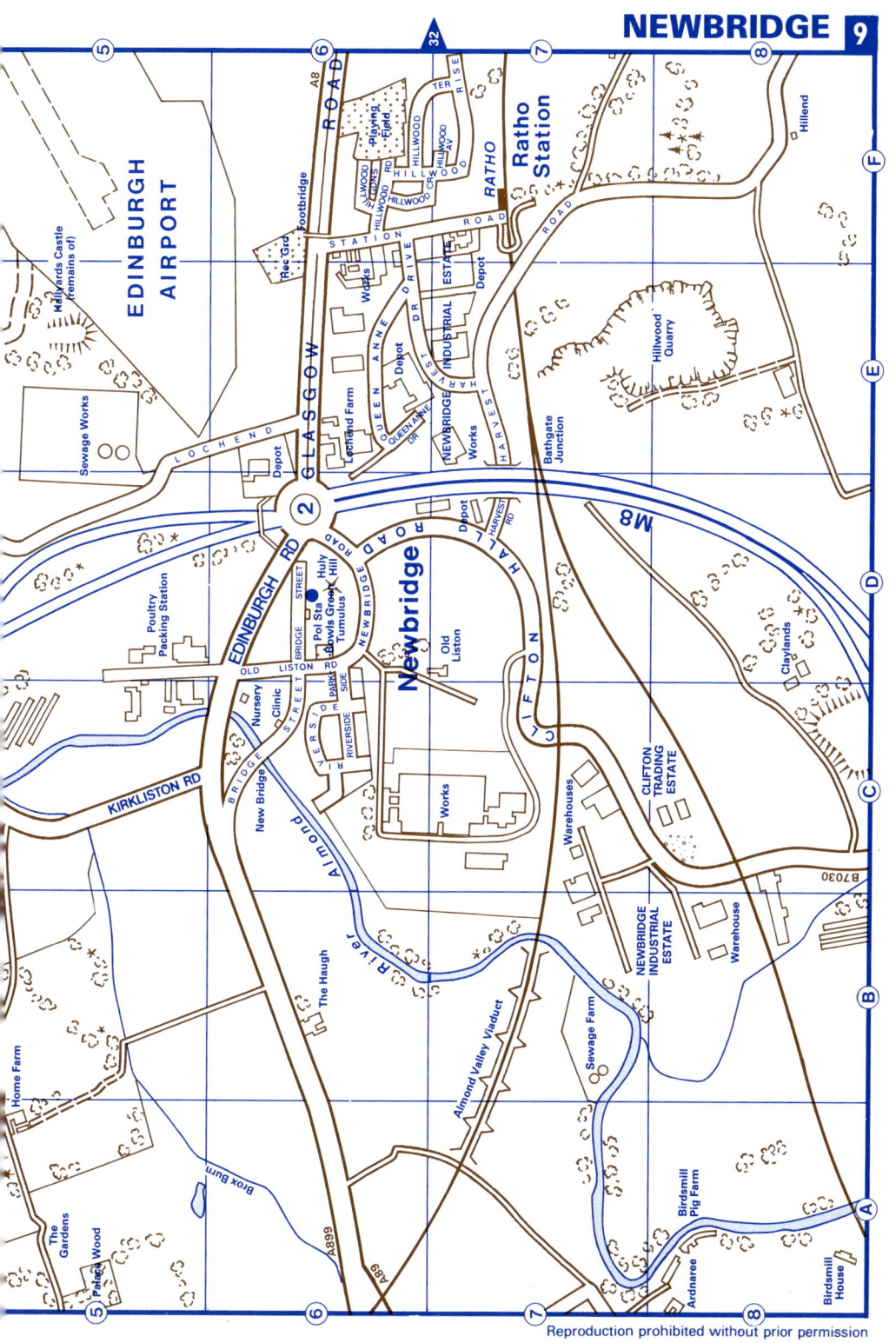

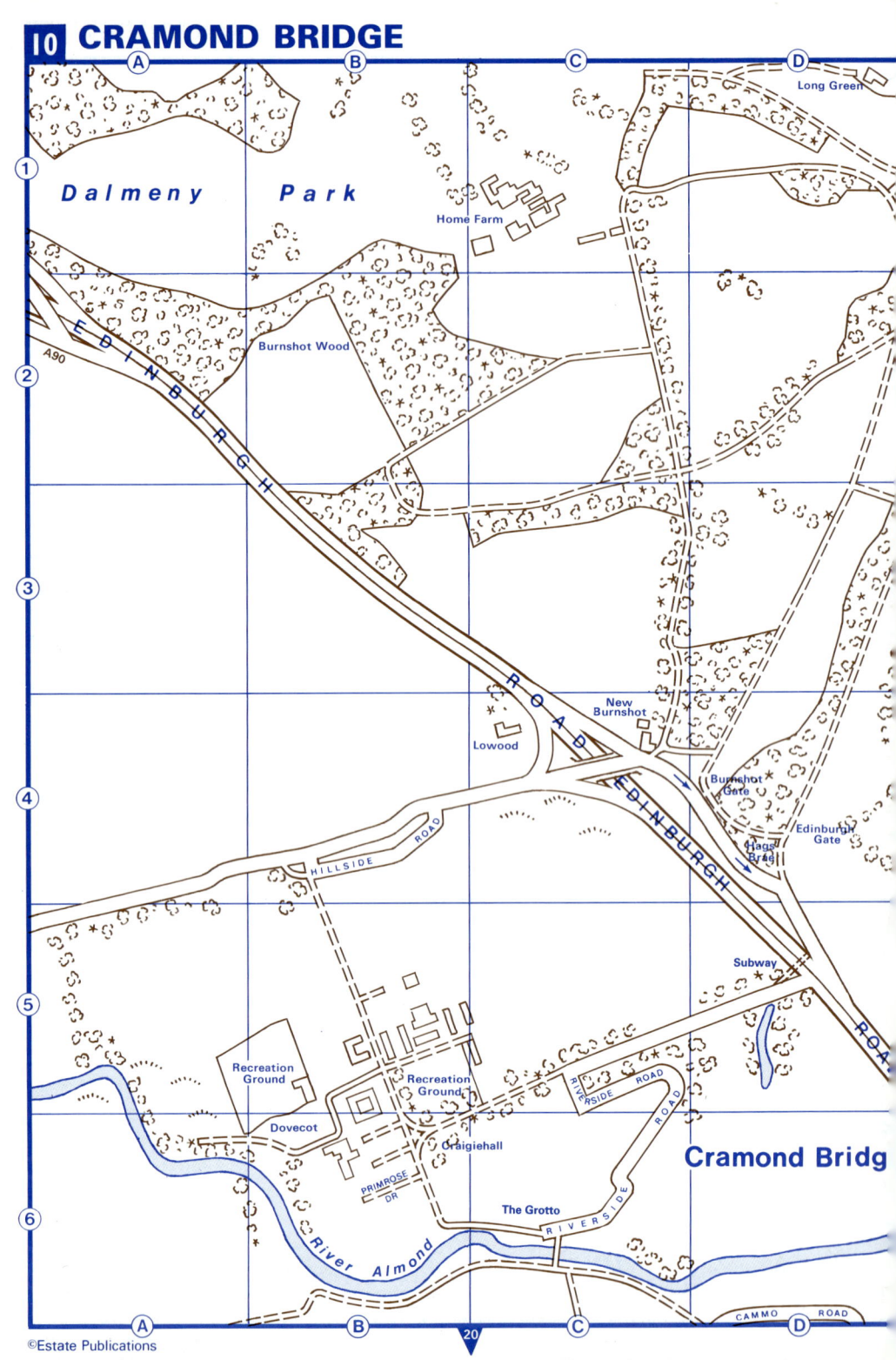

Long Green

Dalmeny Park

Home Farm

EDINBURGH

A90

Burnshot Wood

ROAD

New Burnshot

Lowood

Burnshot Gate

EDINBURGH

Edinburgh Gate

Hags Brae

HILLSIDE   ROAD

Subway

ROAD

Recreation Ground

Recreation Ground

RIVERSIDE   ROAD

ROAD

Cramond Bridg

Dovecot

Craigiehall

PRIMROSE DR

The Grotto

RIVERSIDE

River Almond

CAMMO   ROAD

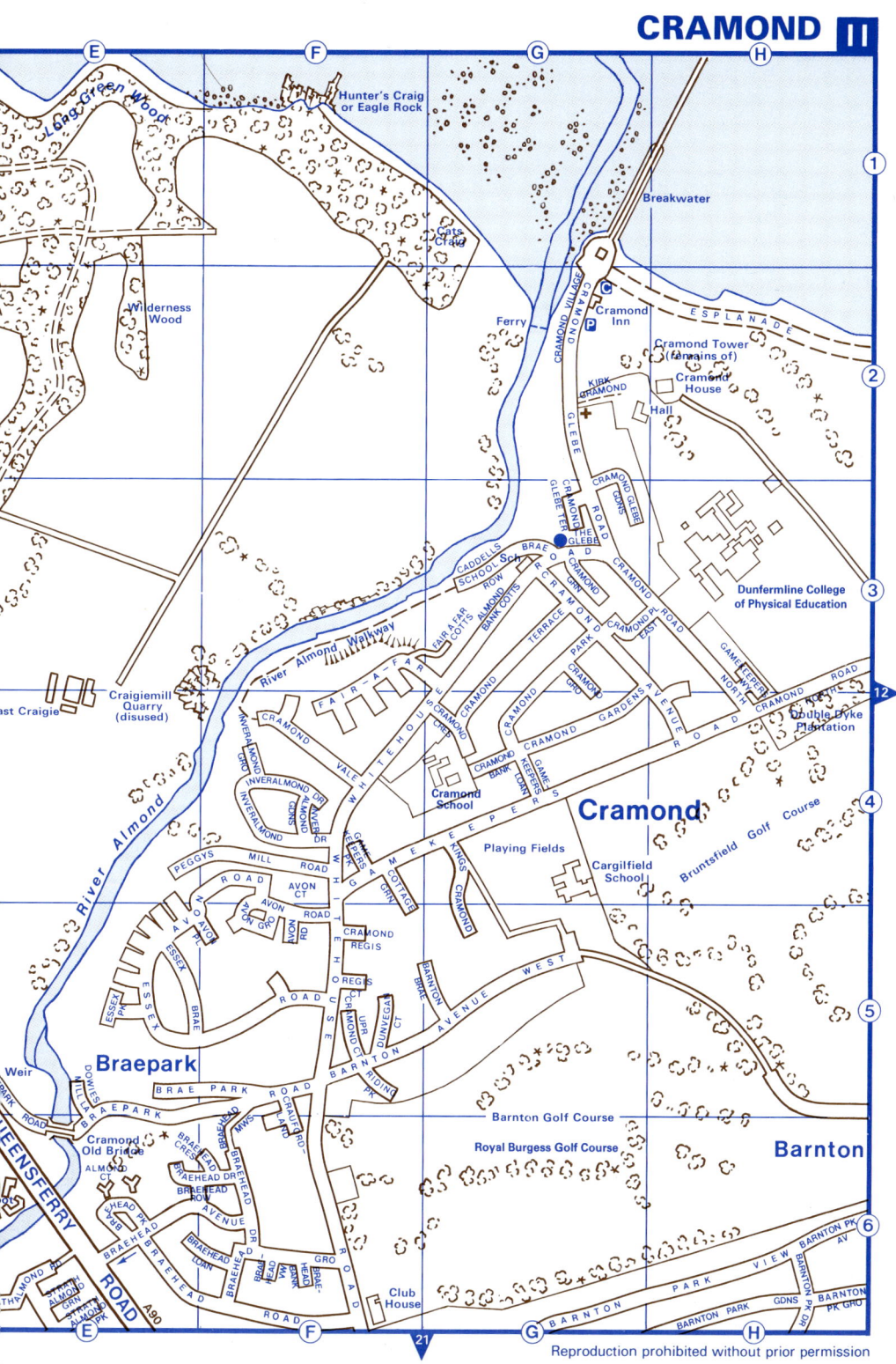

Laug Green Wood

Hunter's Craig or Eagle Rock

Breakwater

Wilderness Wood

Cats Craig

Ferry

Cramond Inn

ESPLANADE

Cramond Tower (remains of)

Cramond House

KIRK CRAMOND

Hall

CRAMOND VILLAGE

GLEBE ROAD

GLEBE TERRACE

CRAMOND GLEBE GDNS

THE GLEBE

Dunfermline College of Physical Education

CADDELLS Sch

SCHOOL BRAE

FAIR-A-FAR COTS

ALMOND BANK COTS

ROW

CRAMOND TERRACE

CRAMOND PARK GRO

CRAMOND PL ROAD EAST

GAMEKEEPERS RD NORTH

CRAMOND RD NORTH

River Almond Walkway

East Craigie

Craigiemill Quarry (disused)

FAIR-A-FAR

WHITEHOUSE RD

CRAMOND CRES

CRAMOND BANK

CRAMOND GARDENS

GAMEKEEPERS

Double Dyke Plantation

River Almond

INVERALMOND DR

INVERALMOND GDNS

INVERALMOND GROVE

CRAMOND VALE

Cramond School

GAMEKEEPERS RD

COTTAGE

KINGS CRAMOND

Cramond

Playing Fields

Cargilfield School

Bruntsfield Golf Course

PEGGYS MILL ROAD

AVON CT

AVON GRO

AVON RD

CRAMOND REGIS

WHITEHOUSE ROAD

KINGS CRAMOND

Weir

ESSEX PK

ESSEX BRAE

ESSEX

UPR CRAMOND CT

REGIS

DUNVEGAN CT

BARNTON BRAE

AVENUE WEST

Braepark

BRAE PARK ROAD

DOWIES MILL LA

BRAEPARK

ROKNLIFF RD

CRAMOND RIDING PK

Cramond Old Bridge

ALMOND CT

BRAEHEAD CRES

BRAEHEAD ROW

BRAEHEAD DR

BRAEHEAD AVENUE

BRAEHEAD

BRAEHEAD PK

BRAEHEAD BANK

BRAEHEAD MWS

BRAEHEAD GRO

BRAEHEAD LOAN

Barnton Golf Course

Royal Burgess Golf Course

Barnton

BARNTON PARK VIEW

BARNTON PK AV

BARNTON PK DR

BARNTON PK GRO

BARNTON GDNS

Club House

BARNTON PARK

QUEENSFERRY ROAD

ALMOND GRN

A90

THY

E F G H

1 2 3 12 4 5 6

21

Silverknowes

Silverknowes Golf Course

Commodore Hotel

ESPLANADE

MARINE DRIVE MARINE DRIVE

Club House

Cramond Rd North

Double Dyke Plantation

Bruntsfield Golf Course

CRAMOND ROAD

Barnton Park Quarry (disused)

Lauriston Castle

Lauriston Farm

Club House

NTHLAWN CT
EASTER PK HO
ROSE CT
STHLAWN CT
WBNK
STHBANK CT
SOUTHBANK

BARNTON

BARNTON LOAN

BARNTON

SOUTH BARNTON AV

EAST BARNTON AV

SAFEWAYS

THE GREEN

SILVERKNOWES

INCHMICKERY CT
OXCARS
MUIRHOUSE

SILVERKNOWES GARDENS
SILVERKNOWES EASTWAY
SILVERKNOWES PL
SILVERKNOWES CRES
SILVERKNOWES AV
SILVERKNOWES ROAD
SILVERKNOWES COURT
SILVERKNOWES GROVE
SILVERKNOWES BANK
SILVERKNOWES HILL
SILVERKNOWES BRAE
SILVERKNOWES DRIVE
SILVERKNOWES TERRACE

MAIN STREET

QUALITY ST

ROSK DELL
CORBIEHILL PL
CORBIEHILL CRESCENT
CORBIEHILL TER
CORBIEHILL AV

VIVIAN TERRACE
CORBIEHILL ROAD
MARCHFIELD

School

Davidsons Mains Park

Davidson's Mains

BARNTON PARK

Oak Plantation

BARNTON PK GRO
BARNTON PARK PL
BARNTON PK DELL
BARNTON PK AV

School

Playing Field

A90

Silverknowes

22

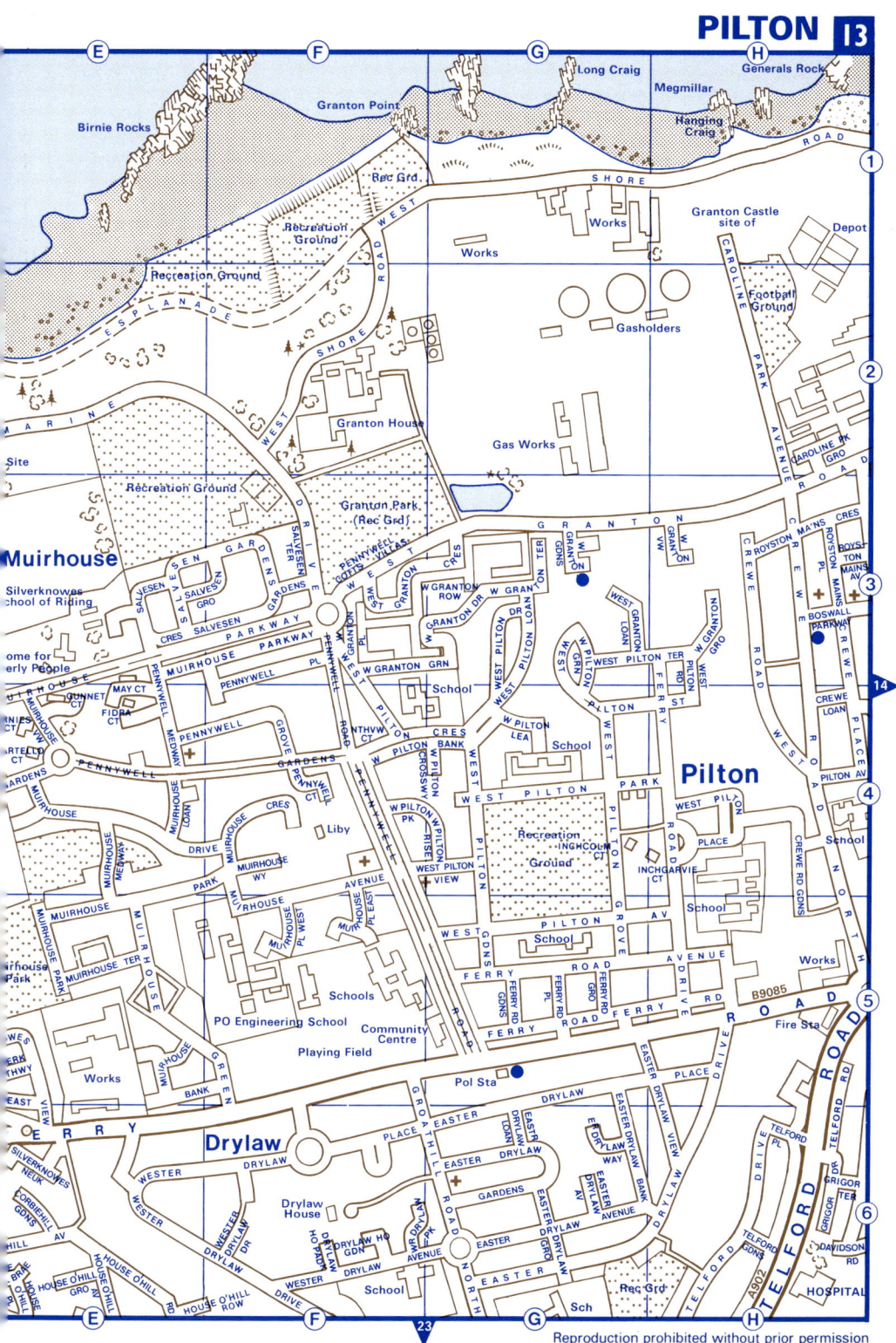

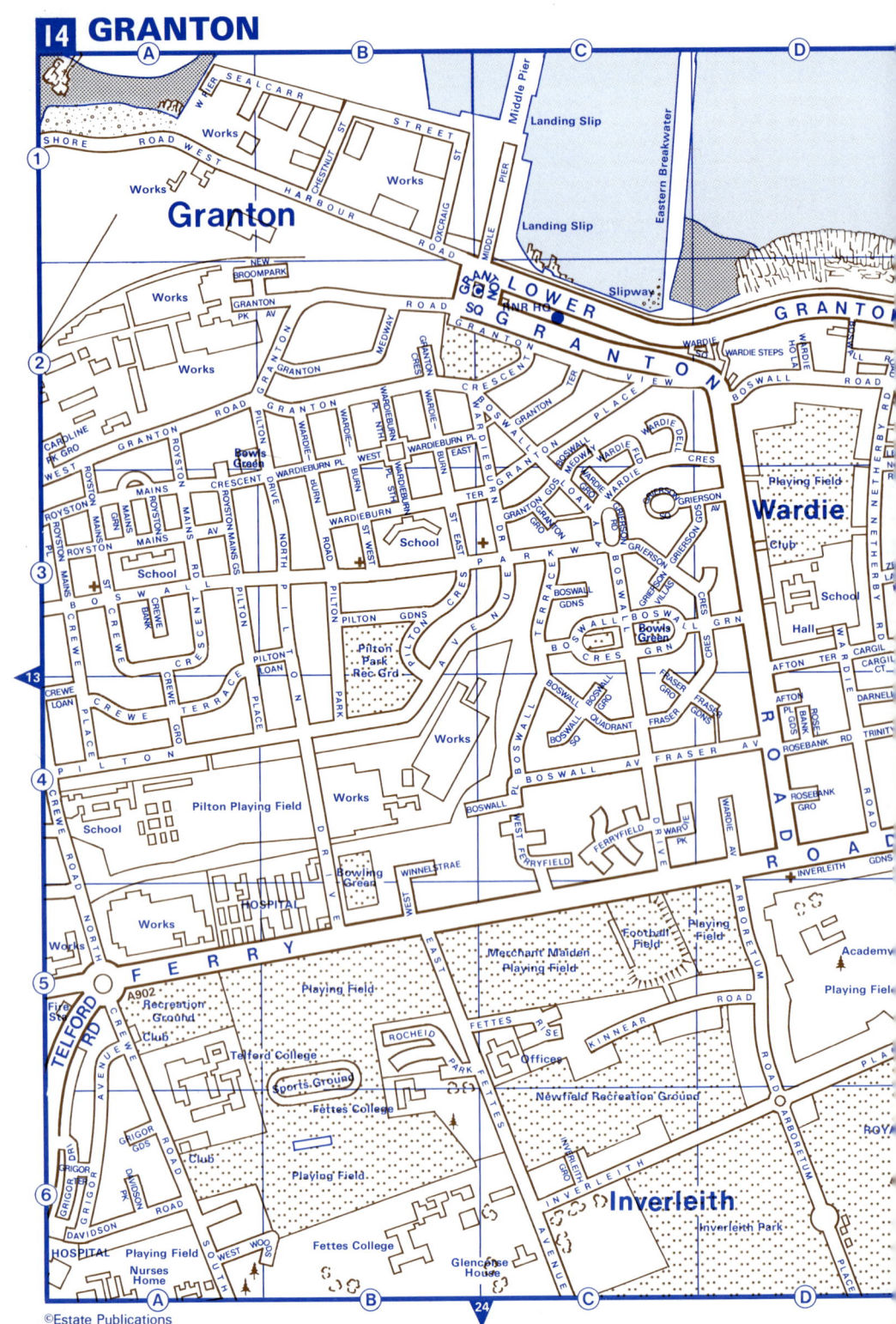

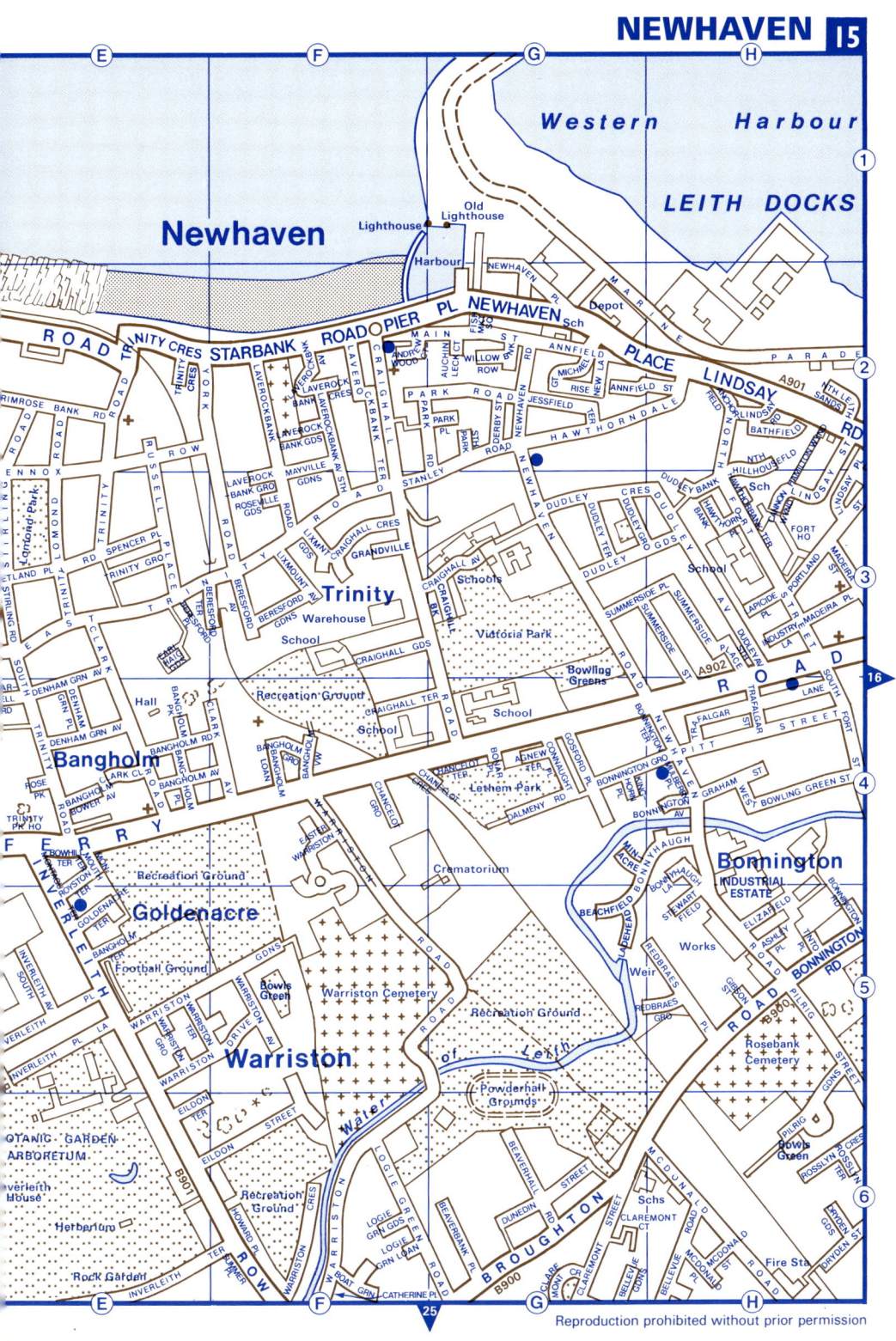

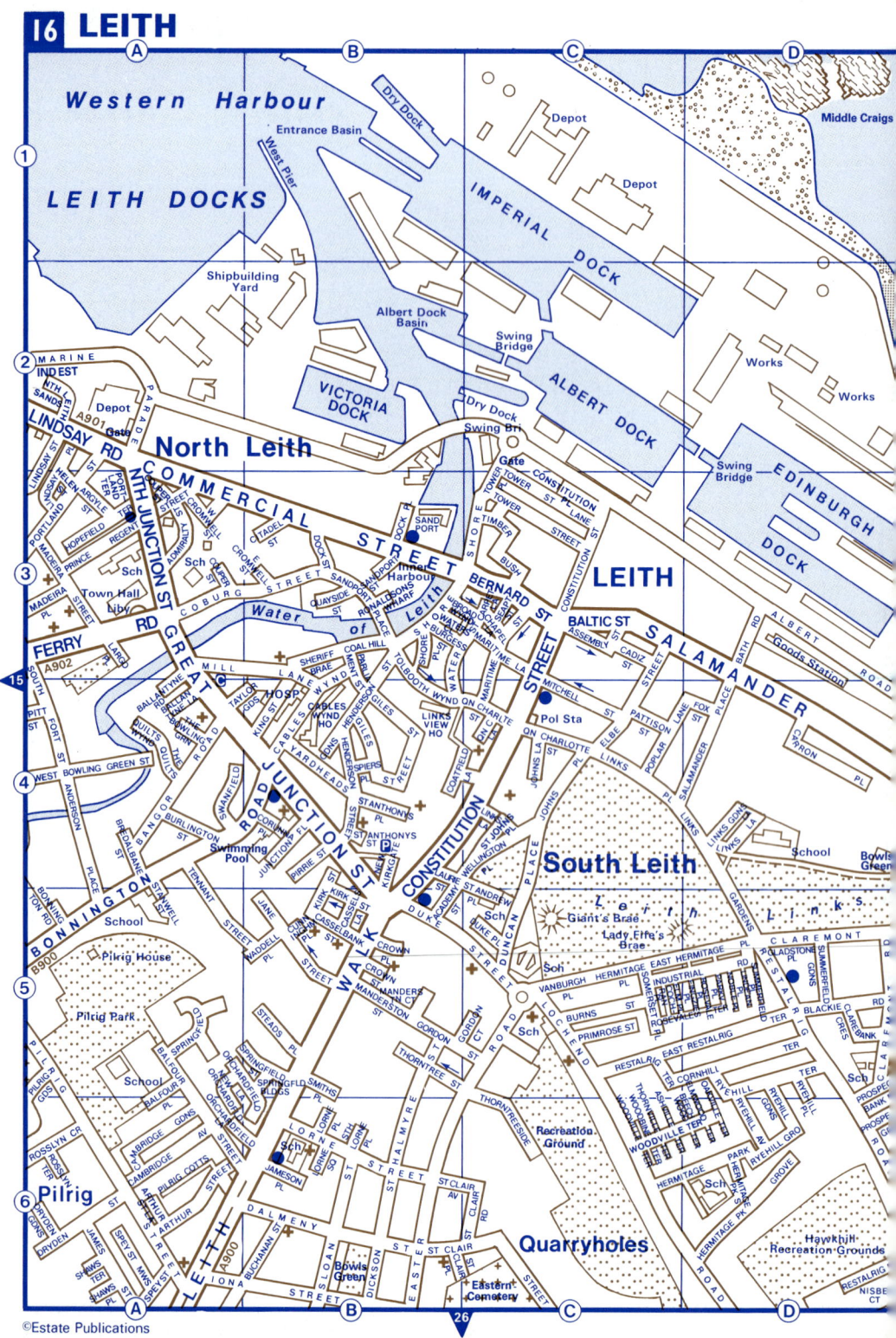

F I R T H   O F   F O R T H

Eastern Craigs

Black Rocks

Eastern Craigs

East Sands of Leith

Pipeline

Works

MARINE ROAD

Goods & Mineral Yard

Pipeline

Sewage Works

ESPLANADE

STREET

SEAFIELD

PARK

SEAFIELD PL.

BOOTHACRE COTTS.

6th Links

BOOTHACRE LA.

PIRNIEFIELD

Seafield Cemetery

Crematorium

laremont Park

REMONT GDS.

Seafield

SEAFIELD

ST

SEACOT

BANK CLO.

BANK TER.

PIRNIEFIELD

PRIES

SPECT BK

ROD

PIRNIEFIELD

TER

PIRNIEFIELD

GRO.

PIRNIEFIELD

BANK

SPECT BANK

RD

PROSPECT

BANK TER

PIRNIEFIELD

PLACE

SEAFIELD

AVENUE

SEAFIELD

ROAD

Works

ROAD

SEAFIELD

PROSPECT

BANK

PROSPECT GRO.

EASTERN GENERAL HOSPITAL

GRAIGENTINNY AVENUE

NORTH

Works

STALRIG

CIRCUS

FINDLAY

CRESCENT

FINDLAY

COTTS

FINDLAY

GARDENS

MEDWAY

FINDLAY

AV.

FINDLAY GRO.

Playing Field

SEAFIELD

ROAD

PROMENADE

RESTALRIG

RESTALRIG SQ.

Craigentinny Golf Course

Club House

GRAIG-ENTINNY

RV.

FILLYSIDE

NANTWICH

DR.

NANTWICH

DRIVE

SEAFIELD

ROAD

SEAFIELD

ROAD

EAST

WAY

A199

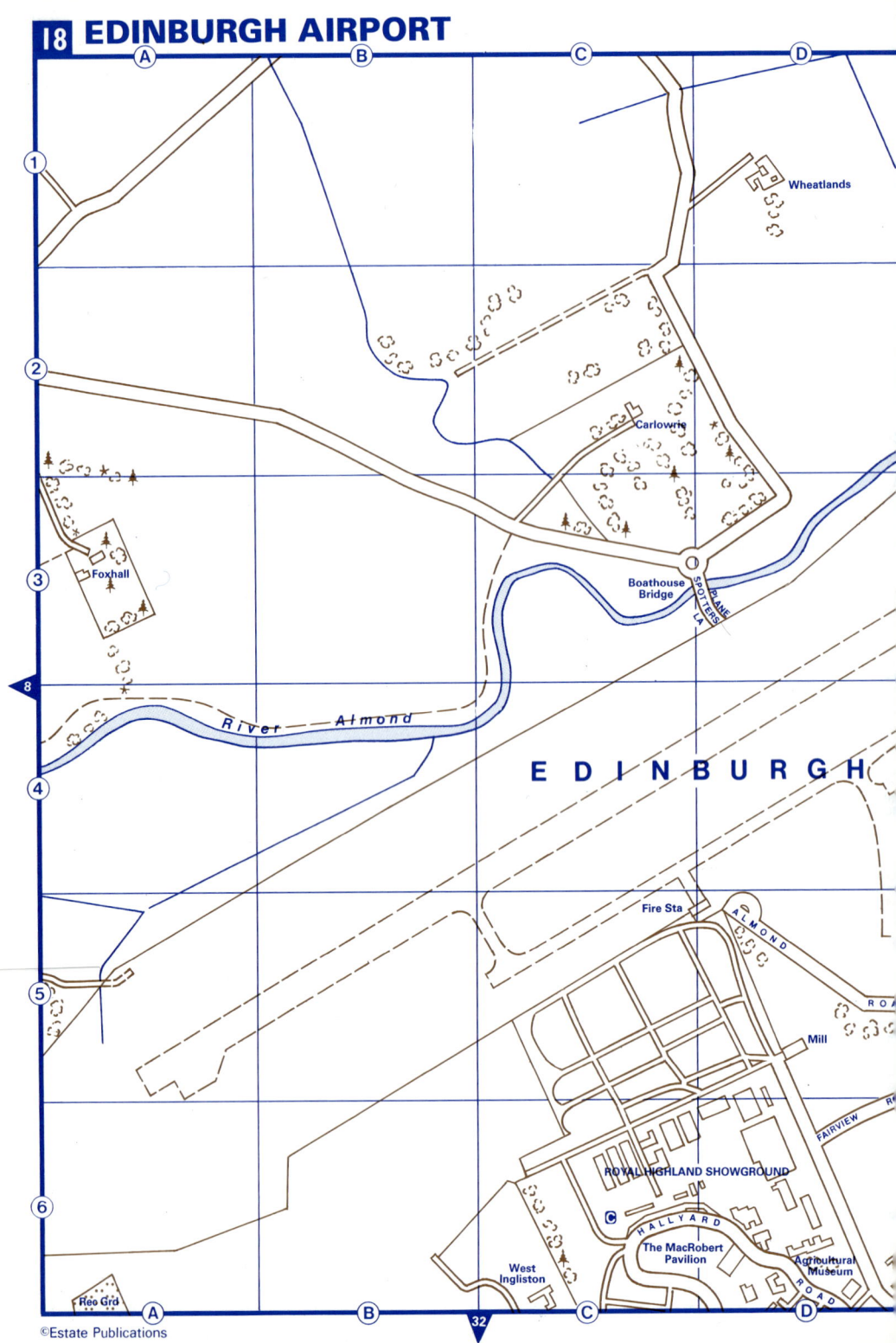

Wheatlands

Carlowrie

Foxhall

Boathouse
Bridge

SPOTTERS LA

River Almond

E D I N B U R G H

Fire Sta

ALMOND

ROA

Mill

FAIRVIEW R

ROYAL HIGHLAND SHOWGROUND

HALLYARD

The MacRobert
Pavilion

Agricultural
Museum

West
Ingliston

Rec Grd

ROAD

E   F   10   G   H

1

Nether Lennie

Old Curling
Pond

River   Almond

2

CAMMO   ROAD

ROAD

Turnhouse

TURNHOUSE   FARM

Turnhouse

3

LENNYMUIR

LENNYMUIR

Playing Field

TURNHOUSE

LENNYMUIR

ROAD

20

(S C O T L A N D)   A I R P O R T

4

TERMINAL
BUILDINGS

JUBILEE   ROAD

P

P

P

Cogar   Burn

5

EASTFIELD   ROAD

JUBILEE

DMOND RD

AV

Pol Sta

MOND

RVIEW   ROAD

Port Royal
Golf Driving Range

Gogar Mains

GOGAR   MAINS   FARM   ROAD

Castle Gogar

6

Castle Gogar
Gardens

st Mains of Ingliston
(Smallholdings)

East Ingliston
House

ROAD

E   F   33   G   H

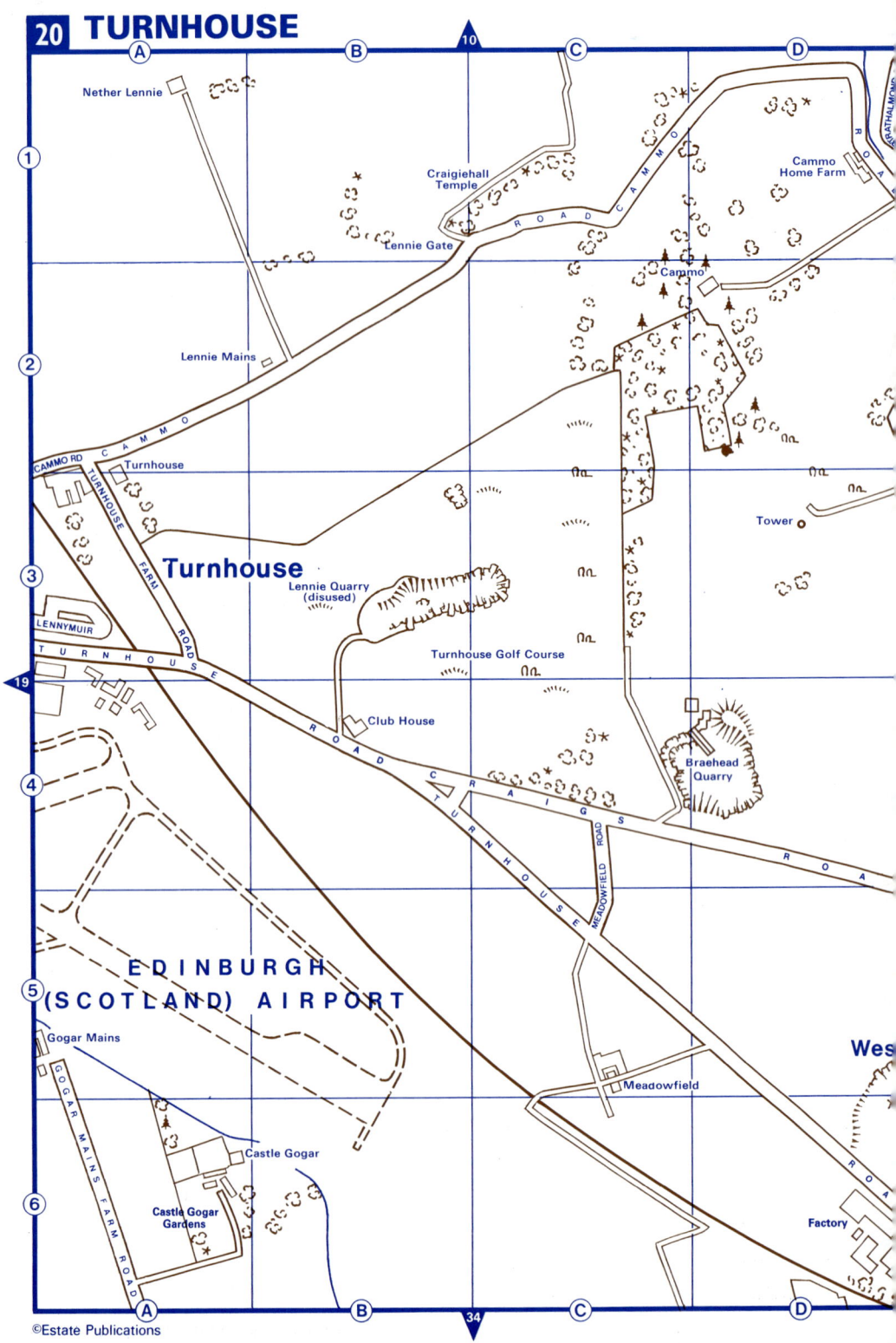

Nether Lennie

Craigiehall Temple

Lennie Gate

Cammo Home Farm

Cammo

Lennie Mains

CAMMO RD

CAMMO ROAD

Turnhouse

Tower

Turnhouse

Lennie Quarry (disused)

LENNYMUIR

TURNHOUSE FARM ROAD

Turnhouse Golf Course

Braehead Quarry

Club House

E D I N B U R G H (S C O T L A N D) A I R P O R T

CRAIGS ROAD

TURNHOUSE ROAD

MEADOWFIELD ROAD

ROAD

Gogar Mains

Wes

Meadowfield

GOGAR MAINS FARM ROAD

Castle Gogar

Castle Gogar Gardens

Factory

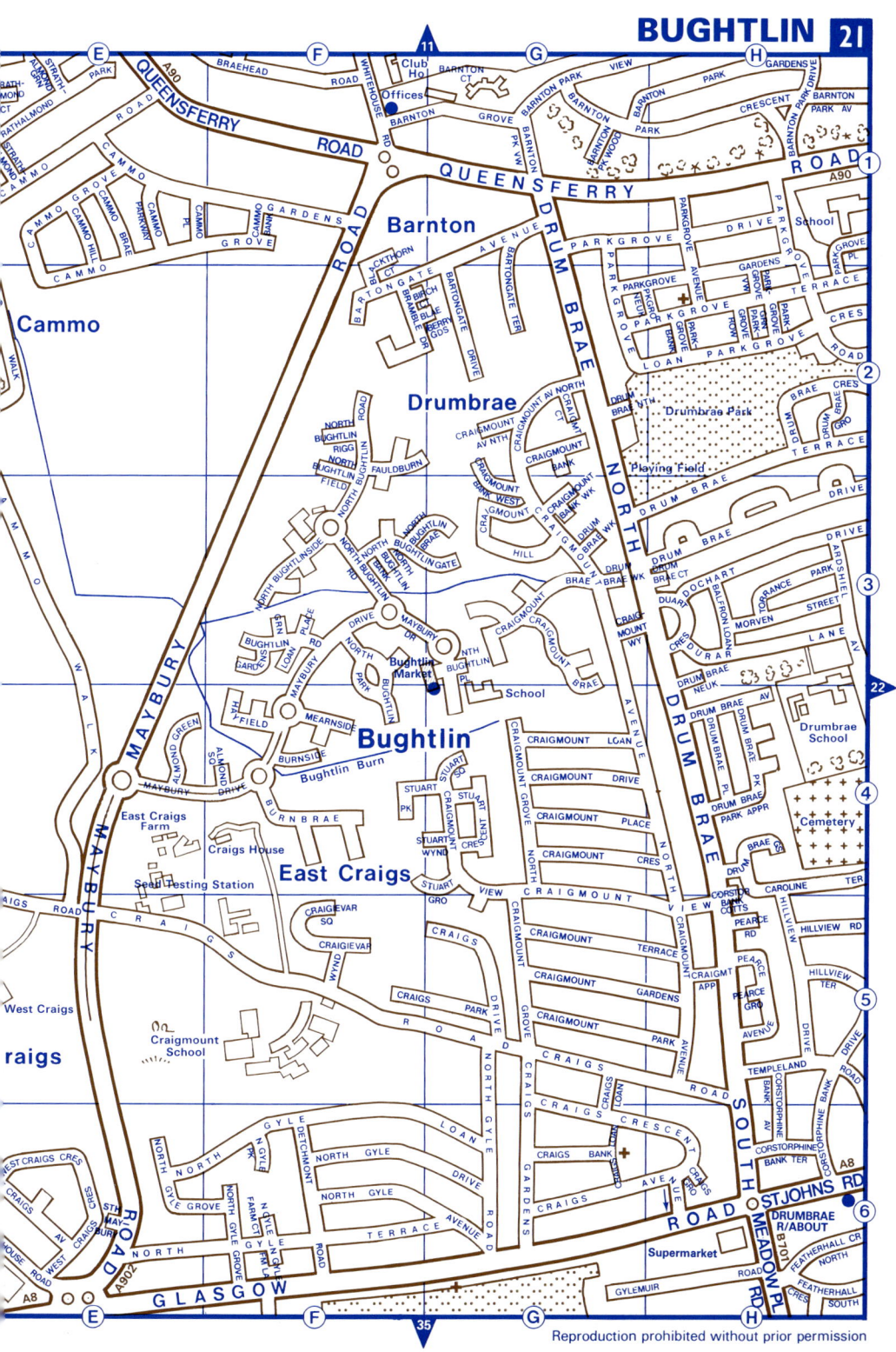

Cammo

Barnton

Drumbrae

Bughtlin

East Craigs

West Craigs

raigs

Drumbrae Park

Playing Field

Drumbrae School

Cemetery

Craigmount School

St.Johns Rd

Drumbrae R/About

Supermarket

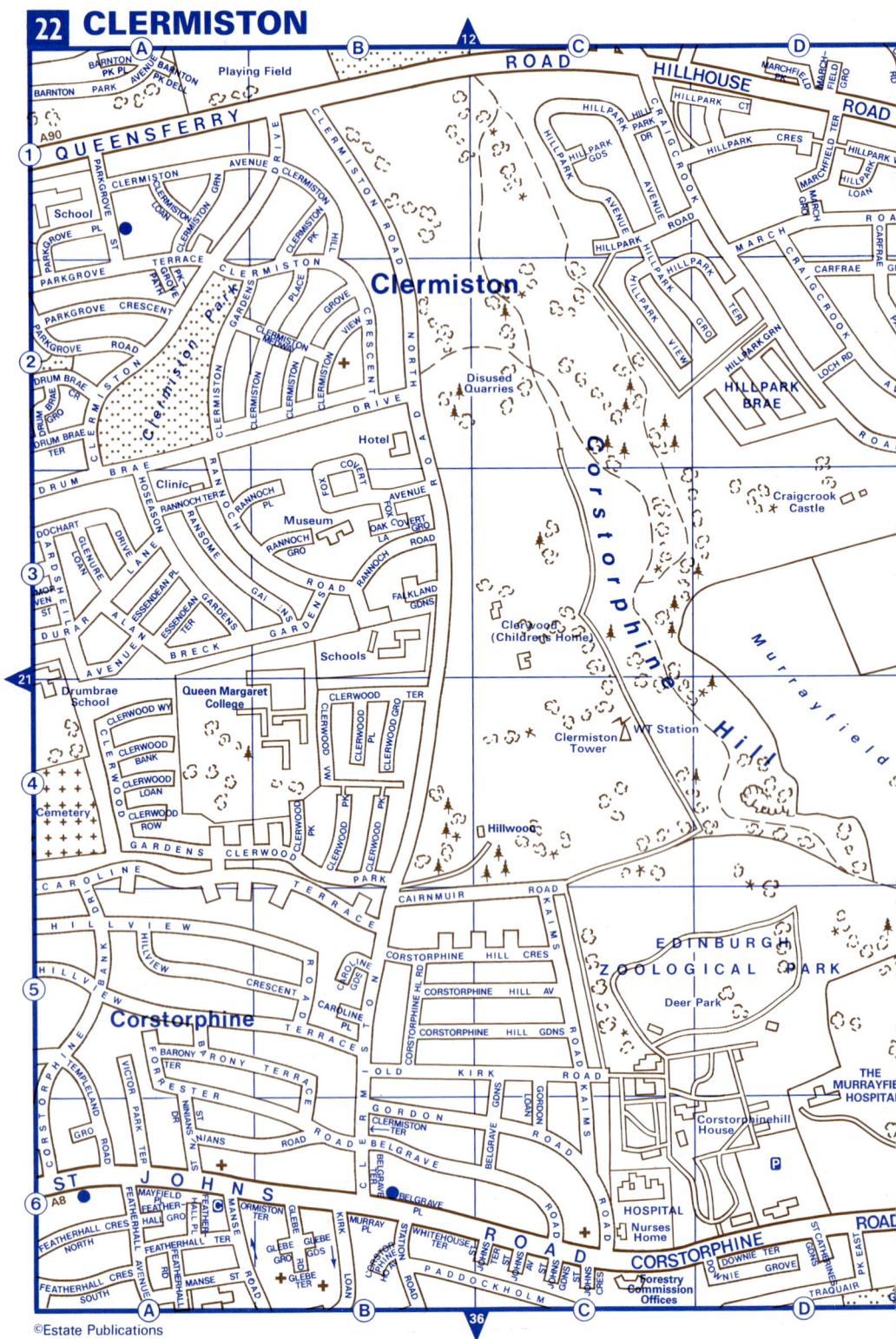

12

CLERMISTON

ROAD

HILLHOUSE ROAD

MARCHFIELD PL

MARCHFIELD GRO

Playing Field

BARNTON PK PL
BARNTON PK AVENUE
BARNTON PK DELL
BARNTON PARK

A90

QUEENSFERRY

CLERMISTON DRIVE

CLERMISTON ROAD

HILLPARK CT

HILLPARK PK DR

HILLPARK GDS

CRAIGCROOK

HILLPARK CRES

MARCHFIELD TER

HILLPARK W

MARCHFIELD GRO

HILLPARK LOAN

School

PARKGROVE
CLERMISTON LOAN
CLERMISTON GRN AVENUE
CLERMISTON AVENUE
CLERMISTON HILL

CLERMISTON

HILLPARK

AVENUE

HILLPARK ROAD

CRAIGCROOK ROAD

MARCH

CARFRAE

LOCH RD

PARKGROVE PL
TERRACE
PK GRO PATH

CLERMISTON PLACE

HILLPARK TER

HILLPARK VIEW

HILLPARK GRN

CARFRAE

PARKGROVE CRESCENT

CLERMISTON GROVE

HILLPARK BRAE

PARKGROVE ROAD

CLERMISTON GARDENS
CLERMISTON MEDWAY
CLERMISTON VIEW

CRESCENT

NORTH

DRIVE

Disused Quarries

Corstorphine Hill

Craigcrook Castle

DRUM BRAE
DRUM BRAE CT
DRUM BRAE TER

CLERMISTON PARK

CLERMISTON TERRACE

Hotel

FOX COVERT AVENUE

DRUM BRAE

HOSEASON
RANNOCH TERZ
RANSOME
DRIVE

Clinic

RANNOCH PL
FOX COVERT

FOX COVERT GRO

Museum
RANNOCH GRO
OAK LA

Clerwood (Childrens Home)

DOCHART
GLENURE LOAN
ARDSHEIL
MORVEN ST
DURAR

ESSENDEAN PL
ESSENDEAN GARDENS
ALAN

RANNOCH ROAD

RANNOCH ROAD

FALKLAND GDNS

Murrayfield

21

AVENUE
BRECK GARDENS
GAIN S GARDENS

ROAD

Schools

Clermiston Tower

WT Station

Drumbrae School

Queen Margaret College

CLERWOOD WY
CLERWOOD
CLERWOOD BANK
CLERWOOD LOAN
CLERWOOD ROW

CLERWOOD TER
CLERWOOD PL
CLERWOOD GRO

Cemetery

GARDENS

CLERWOOD PK

CLERWOOD

CLERWOOD PK

Hillwood

CAROLINE

TERRACE

PARK

CAIRNMUIR ROAD

EDINBURGH

HILLVIEW
HILLVIEW
Corstorphine

CRESCENT

CAROLINE GDS
CAROLINE PL
CAROLINE TERRACE

CORSTORPHINE HILL RD

CORSTORPHINE HILL CRES

CORSTORPHINE HILL AV

CORSTORPHINE HILL GDNS

KAIMS

ZOOLOGICAL PARK

Deer Park

THE MURRAYFIELD HOSPITAL

HILLVIEW BANK

TEMPLELAND GRO
VICTOR PARK TER
FORRESTER
ST NINIANS DR
ST NINIANS ROAD

BARONY TER
BARONY TERRACE
FORRESTER

OLD KIRK ROAD

GORDON TER
CLERMISTON TER

BELGRAVE GDNS

GORDON LOAN

GORDON ROAD

KAIMS ROAD

Corstorphinehill House

P

Corstorphine

CLERMISTON ROAD

BELGRAVE ROAD

BELGRAVE PL

HOSPITAL
Nurses Home

ST JOHNS

A8

MAYFIELD
FEATHERHALL
HALL PL
ORMISTON TER
MANSE

GLEBE TER
GLEBE GRO
GLEBE RD
GLEBE GDS

MURRAY PL

BELGRAVE

ROAD

CORSTORPHINE

DOWNIE TER
DOWNIE GROVE

ROAD

FEATHERHALL CRES NORTH

FEATHERHALL AVENUE
FEATHERHALL TER

MANSE ST

KIRK LOAN

PADDOCKHOLM

WHITEHOUSE TER

JOHNS
JOHNS GDNS
JOHNS CRES

Forestry Commission Offices

TRAQUAIR PK EAST
ST CATHERINES GDNS

FEATHERHALL CRES SOUTH

36

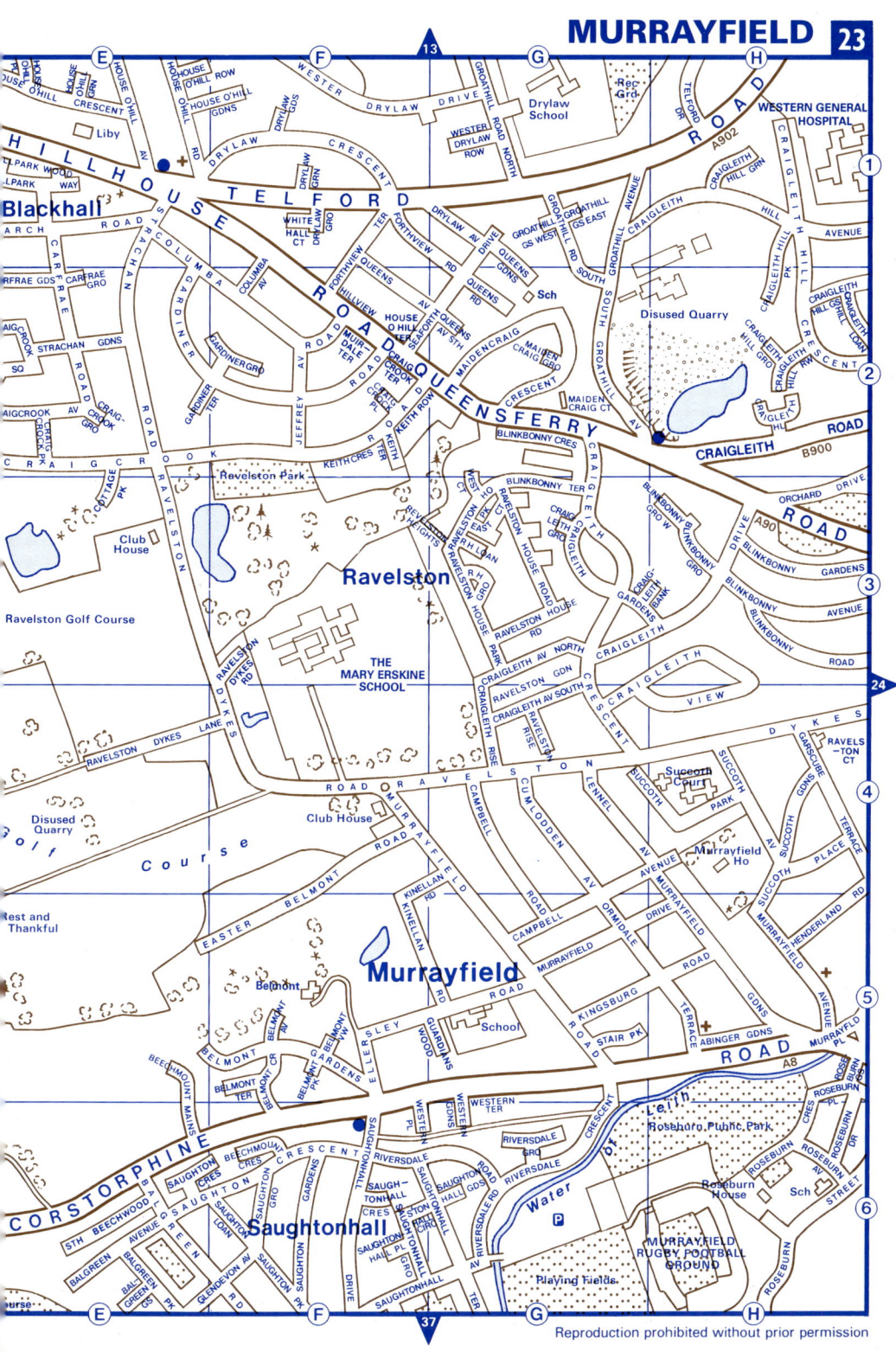

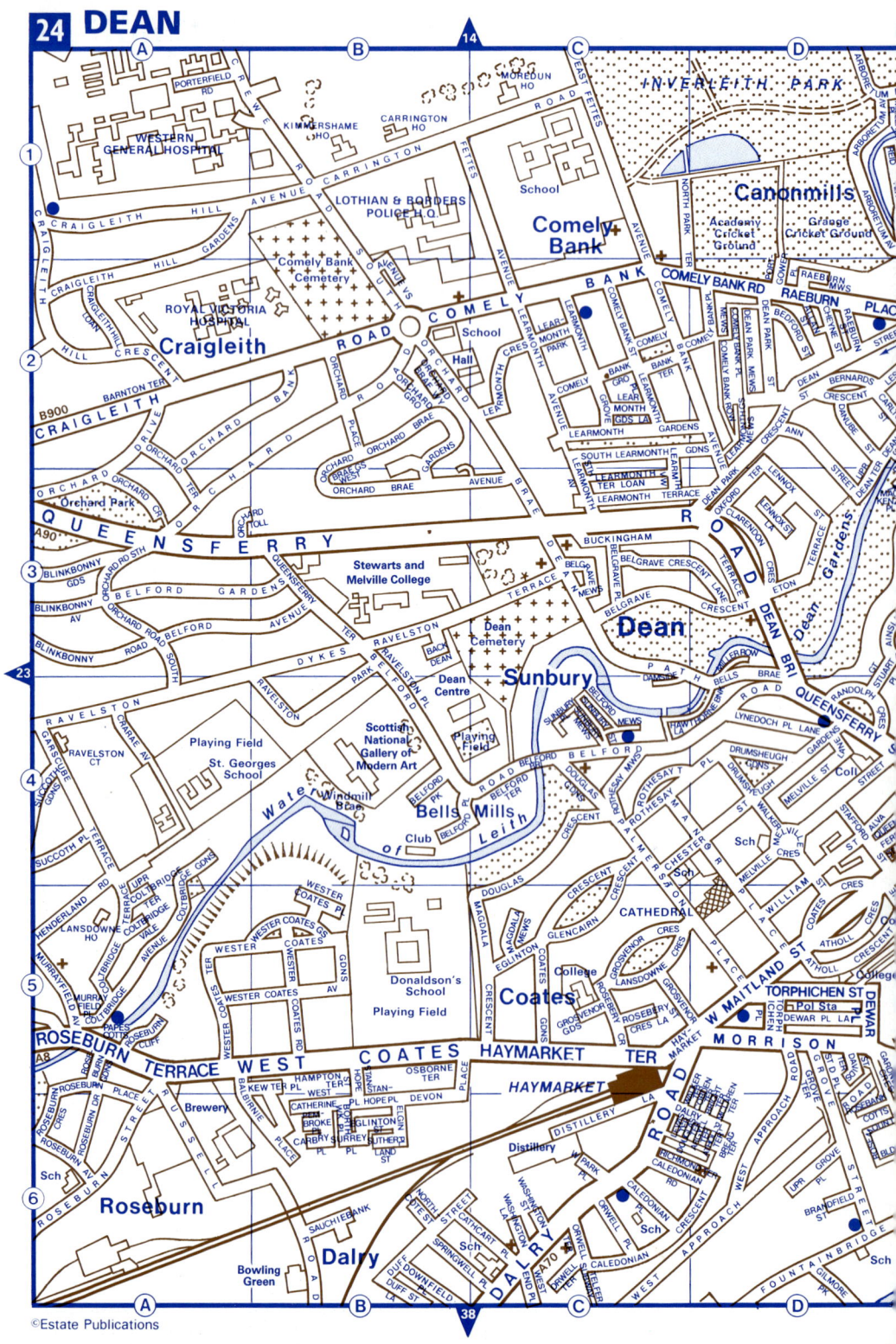

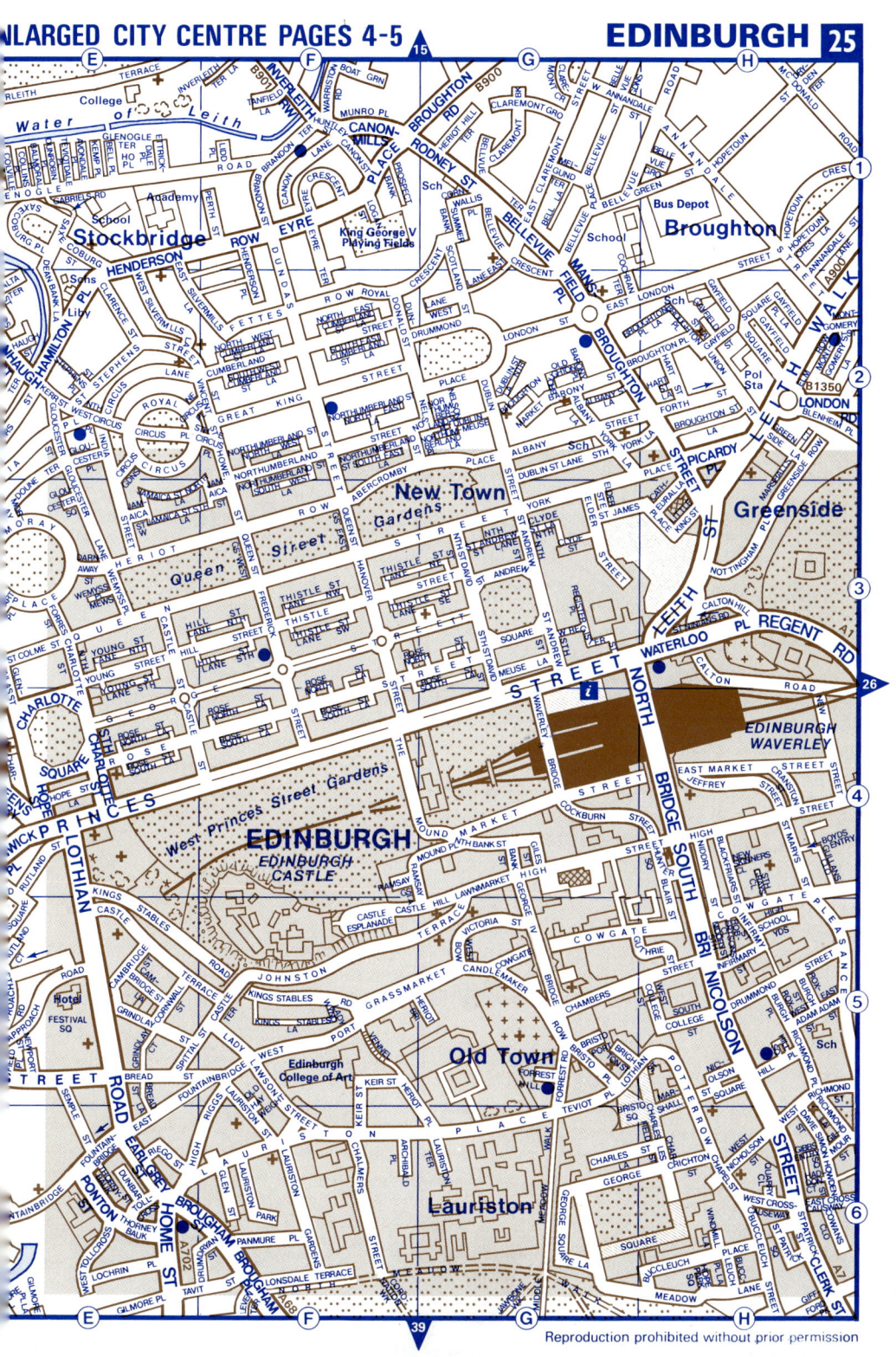

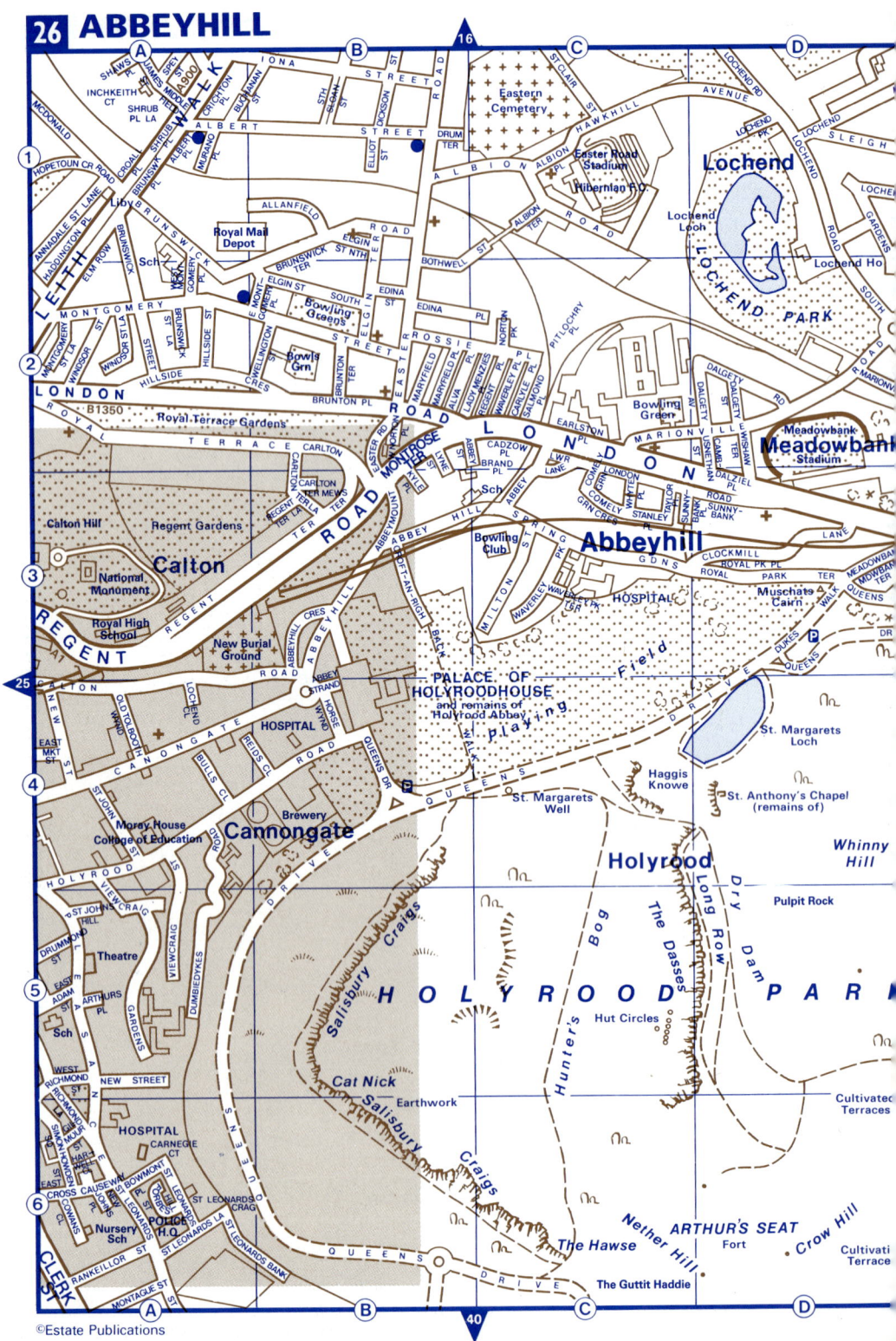

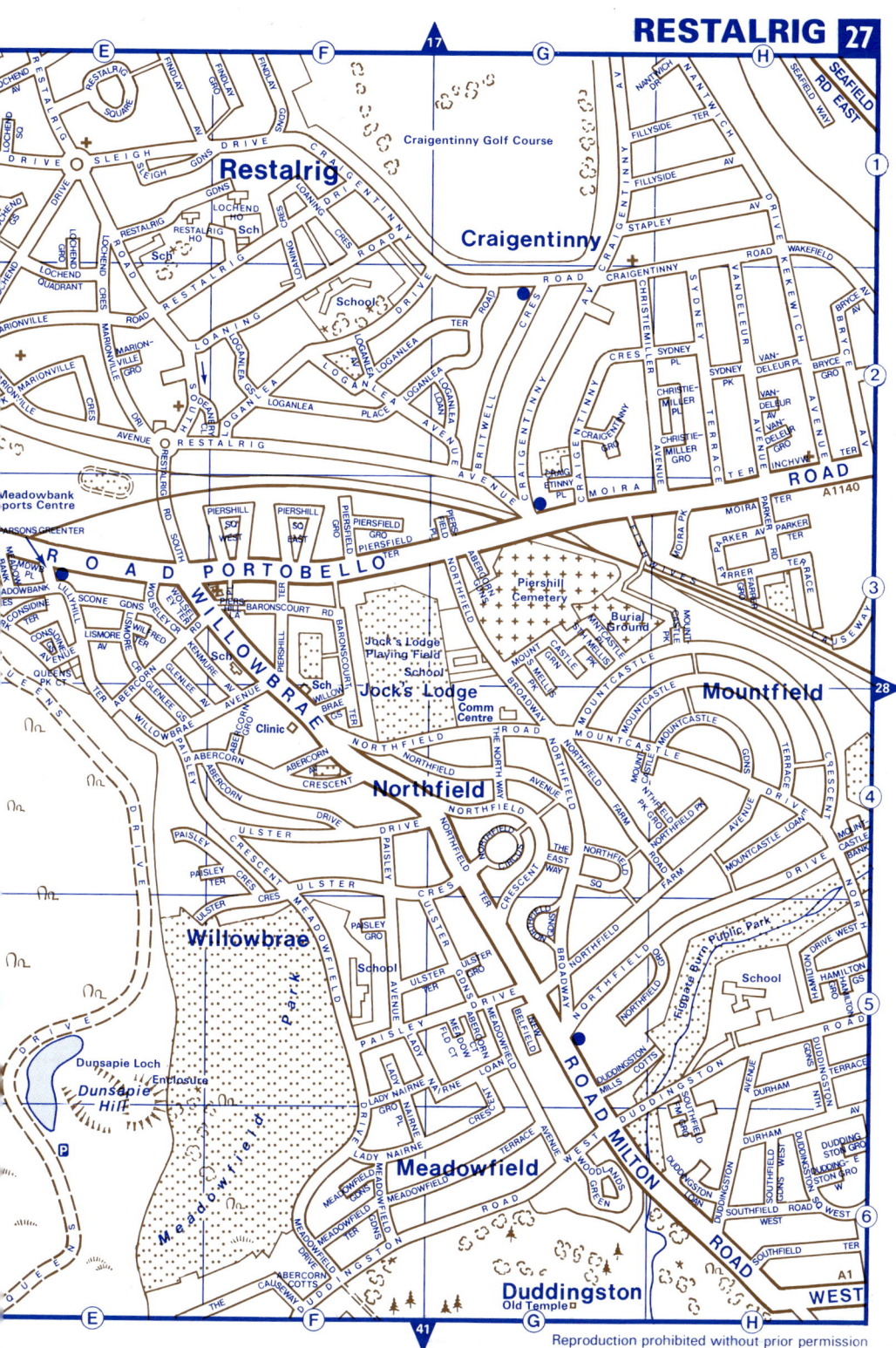

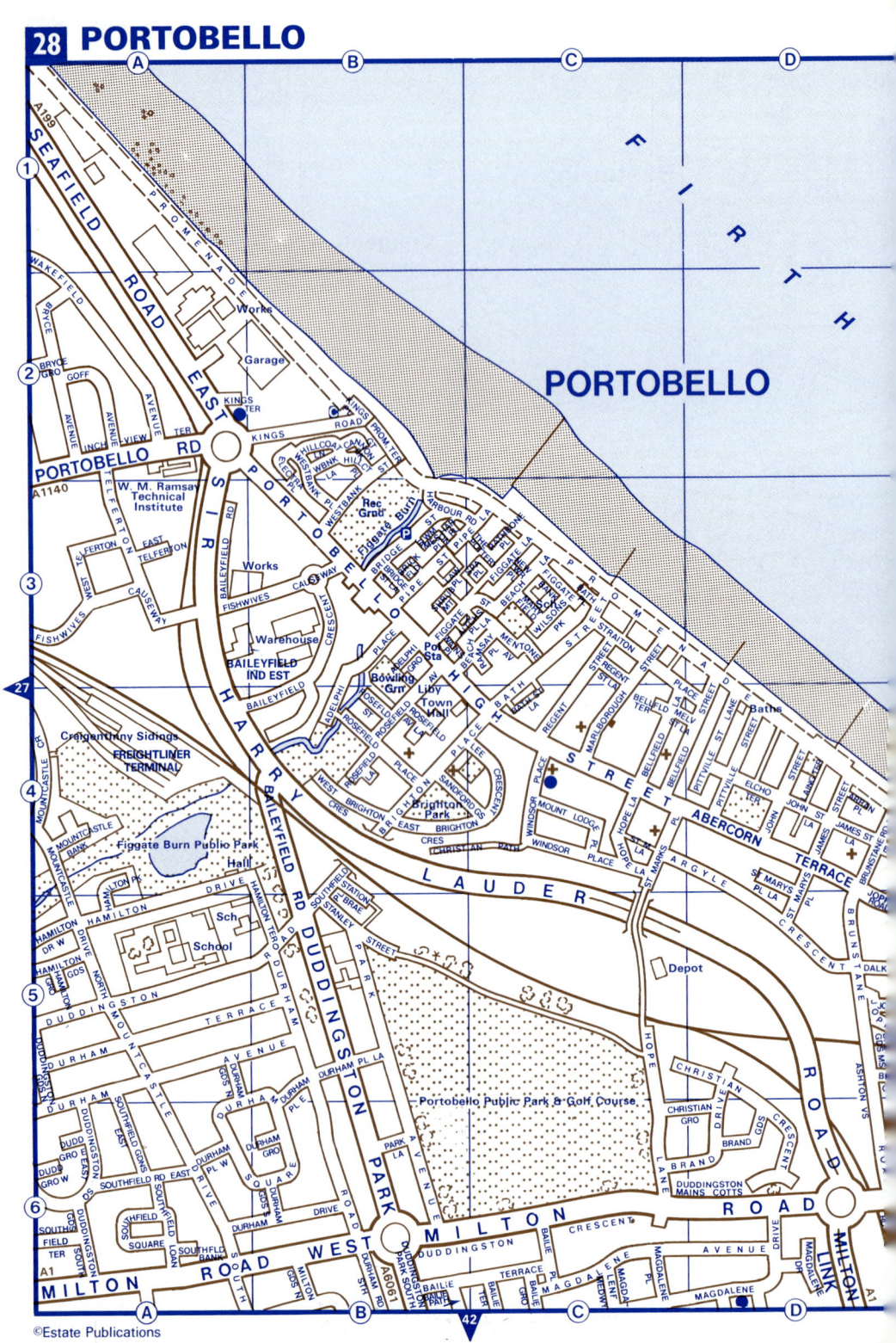

PORTOBELLO

FIRTH

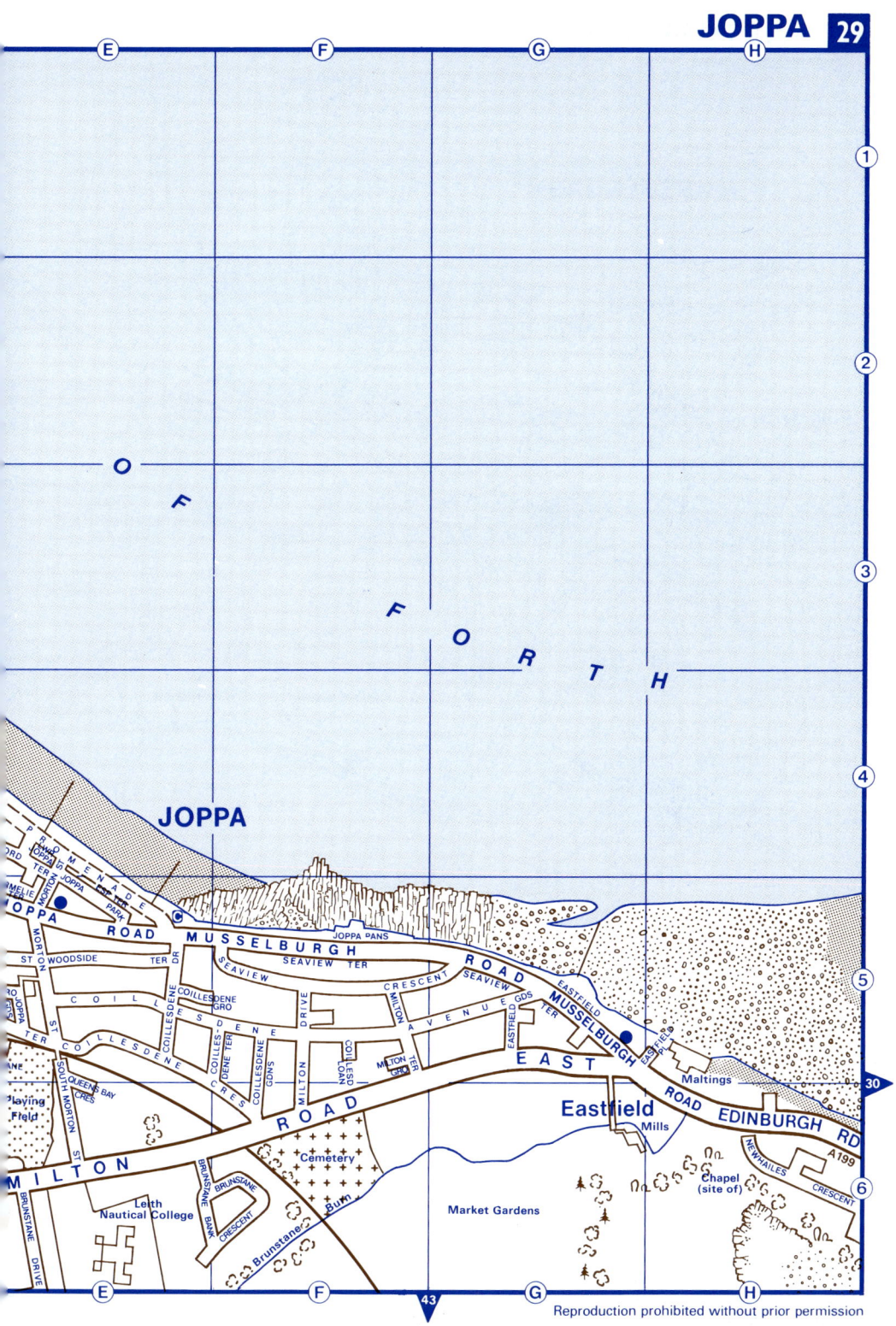

JOPPA

O F

F O R T H

EASTFIELD

MUSSELBURGH ROAD

SEAVIEW TER

MILTON AVENUE

EAST ROAD EDINBURGH RD

Eastfield

Maltings

Mills

Market Gardens

Cemetery

Leith Nautical College

Chapel (site of)

NEWHAILES CRESCENT

A199

Playing Field

MILTON ROAD

BRUNSTANE DRIVE

Brunstane Burn

QUEENS BAY

COILLESDENE

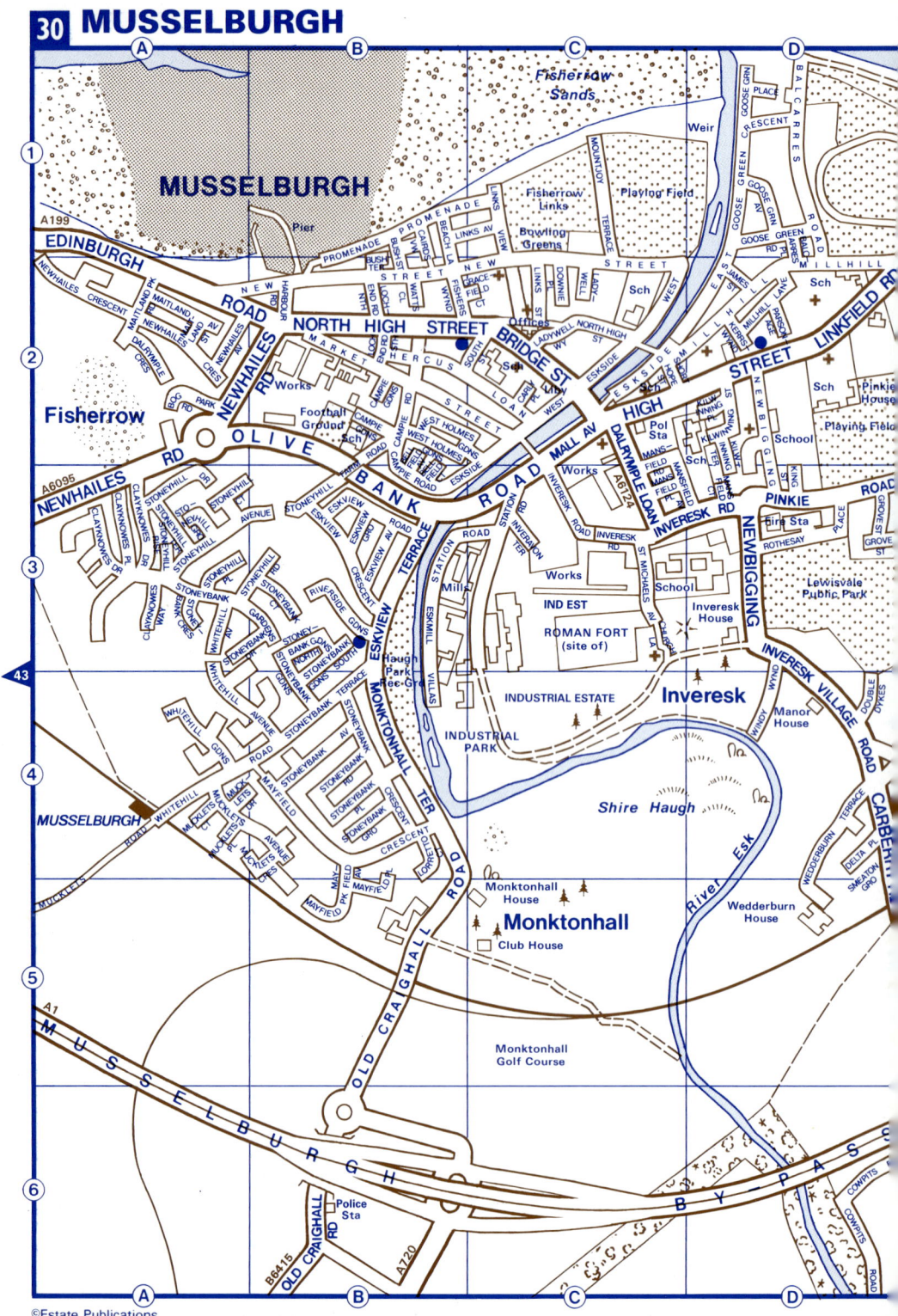

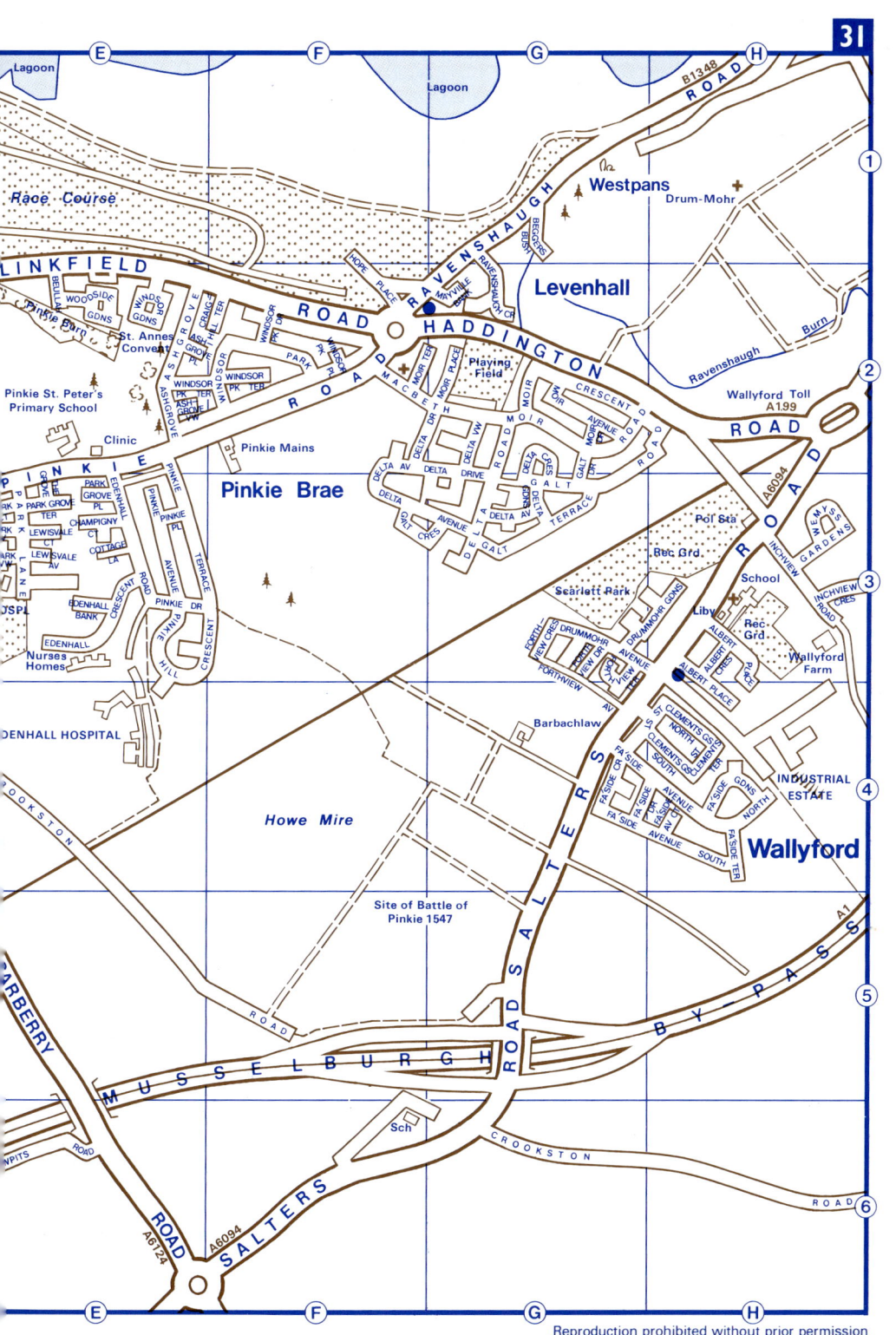

Lagoon

Lagoon

Lagoon

B1348

ROAD

E F G H

1

Race Course

Westpans

Drum-Mohr

LINKFIELD

WOODSIDE
GDNS
BELLULA
Pinkie Burn
WINDSOR
GDNS
St. Annes
Convent
CRAIG HILL TER
ASH GROVE
WINDSOR GROVE
WINDSOR PL
PARK
WINDSOR PK TER
WINDSOR VW

HOPE PLACE

ROAD
RAVENSHAUGH
HADDINGTON

MAYVILLE
PARK
MAYVILLE
RAVENSHAUGH CR
BEGGARS BUSH

Levenhall

Ravenshaugh

Burn

2

Pinkie St. Peter's
Primary School

ASHGROVE
WINDSOR
PK TER
WINDSOR
PK
WINDSOR
VW

ROAD

MACBETH
MOIR TER
MOIR PLACE

Playing
Field

MOIR
MOIR
MOIR
AVENUE
CRESCENT
MOIR
CRES
GALT
VW
GALT
GALT TER

ROAD

CRESCENT
ROAD

Wallyford Toll
A1.99

ROAD

A6094

1

Clinic

PINKIE

Pinkie Mains

Pinkie Brae

PINKIE PL
PINKIE AVENUE
PINKIE TERRACE
PINKIE DR
PINKIE HILL
PINKIE CRESCENT

DELTA AV
DELTA
DELTA
DRIVE
DELTA VW
DELTA
DELTA
GALT CRES
GALT CRES
DELTA AV
DELTA
DELTA AV
DELTA
GALT
TERRACE

Pol Sta

Rec Grd.

School

WEMYSS
GARDENS

INCHVIEW
CRES

3

PARK
GROVE
PL
EDENHALL
TER
CHAMPIGNY
GROVE
LEWISVALE
CT
LEWISVALE
AV
COTTAGE
LA
CRESCENT
ROAD
EDENHALL
BANK

Scarlett Park

FORTH VIEW CRES
FORTH VIEW DR
FORTHVIEW
AV
DRUMMOHR
DRUMMOHR GDNS
DRUMMOHR
AVENUE
INCHVIEW

Liby

ALBERT
ALBERT
PLACE
ALBERT
CRES
ALBERT
PL
Rec
Grd

INCHVIEW
ROAD

Wallyford
Farm

Nurses
Homes

EDENHALL

ALBERT PLACE

EDENHALL HOSPITAL

Barbachlaw

Howe Mire

SALTERS

FA SIDE
FA SIDE CR
FA SIDE
AVENUE
FA SIDE
FA SIDE
AVENUE
SOUTH
ST CLEMENTS GN
ST CLEMENTS GN
NORTH
ST CLEMENTS GN
SOUTH
FA SIDE GDNS
NORTH
FA SIDE
GDNS
NORTH
FA SIDE TER

INDUSTRIAL
ESTATE

Wallyford

4

CROOKSTON

Site of Battle of
Pinkie 1547

ROAD

BY-PASS

A1

5

ARBERRY

MUSSELBURGH

ROAD

SALTERS

Sch

CROOKSTON

PITS
ROAD

ROAD

A6094
A6124

SALTERS

ROAD

6

E F G H

Reproduction prohibited without prior permission

A8

GLASGOW ROAD

West Ingliston

HALLYARD ROAD

Rec Grd

Footbridge

Works

QUEEN ANNE DR

HARVEST DRIVE

HILLWOOD GDS

HILLWOOD

HILLWOOD RD

HILLWOOD CRES

Playing Field

HILLWOOD

Ratho Station

HILLWOOD TER

HILLWOOD AV

RISE

Depot

Primary School

HARVEST

RATHO

ROAD

Norton Mair

Norton Hotel

Hillwood Quarry

BAIRD ROAD

Hillend

Ratho Byres

Works

Freelands

Burial Ground

Hall

FREELANDS

BAIRD

Ratho Hall

Kirkton Farm

UNION CANAL

Craigpark

HALLCROFT GDN

HALLCROFT

HALLCROFT CL

HALLCROFT NEUK

HALL-CROFT CT

HALLCROFT PARK

CRAIGPARK

CRAIGPARK CRES

HALLCROFT RISE

NORTH

SCHOOL

AVENUE

ROAD

MAIN

HILLVIEW

STREET

WYNDA

School

Bowling Green

WEST CROFT

EAST CROFT

Playing Field

CROFT

PARK

ROAD

Ratho Park Gardens

Street

DALMAHOY

Ratho

LUMSDEN CT

HILLVIEW COTTS

COTTAGES

Pol Sta

WILKIESTON ROAD

ROAD

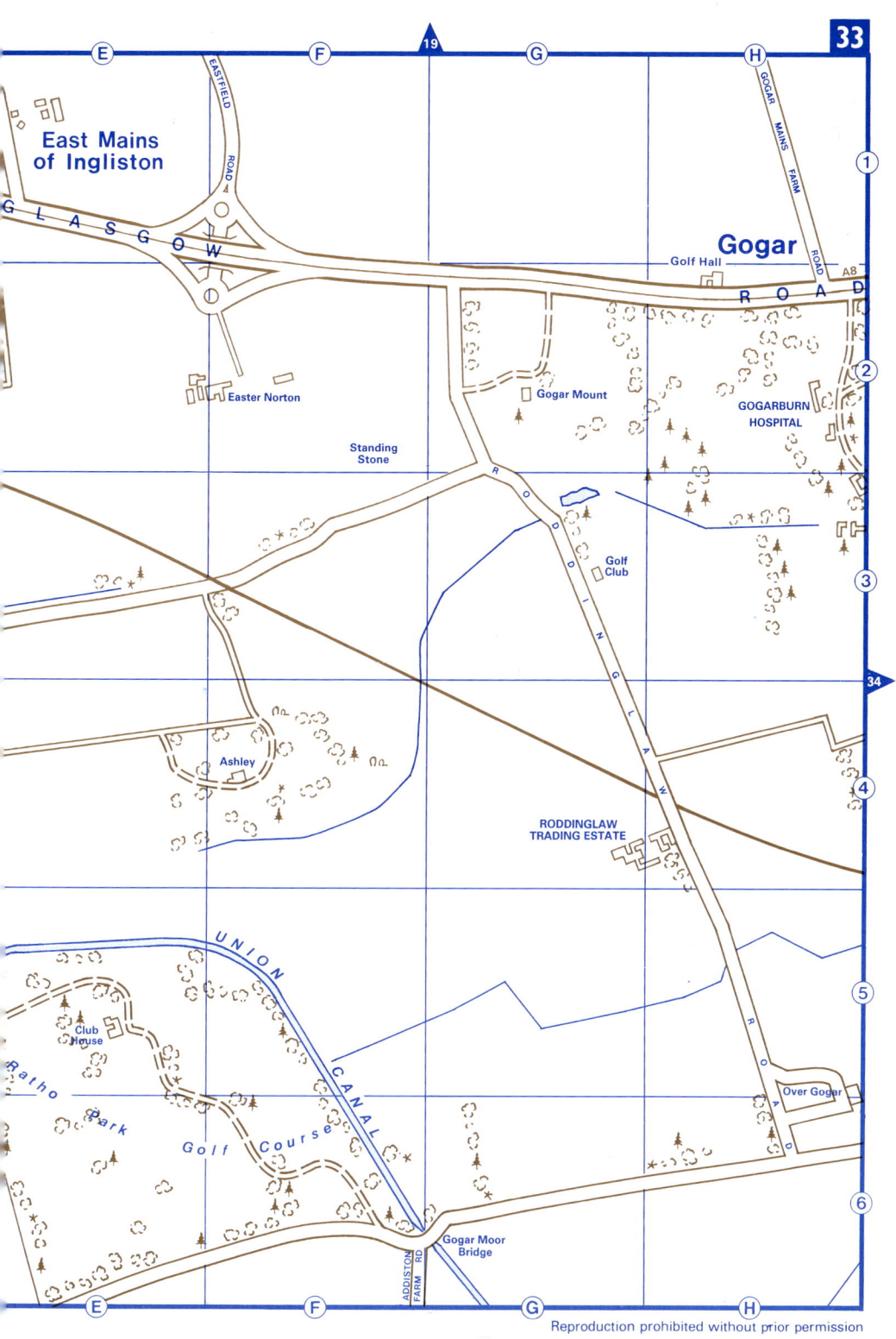

33

E F 19 G H

① East Mains of Ingliston

EASTFIELD ROAD

G L A S G O W

Gogar

Golf Hall

GOGAR MAINS FARM ROAD A8

R O A D

②

Easter Norton

Gogar Mount

GOGARBURN HOSPITAL

Standing Stone

R O D D I N G L A W

Golf Club

③

34

Ashley

RODDINGLAW TRADING ESTATE

④

U N I O N

⑤

Club House

Ratho Park

R O A D

Over Gogar

CANAL

Golf Course

⑥

Gogar Moor Bridge

ADDISTON FARM RD

E F G H

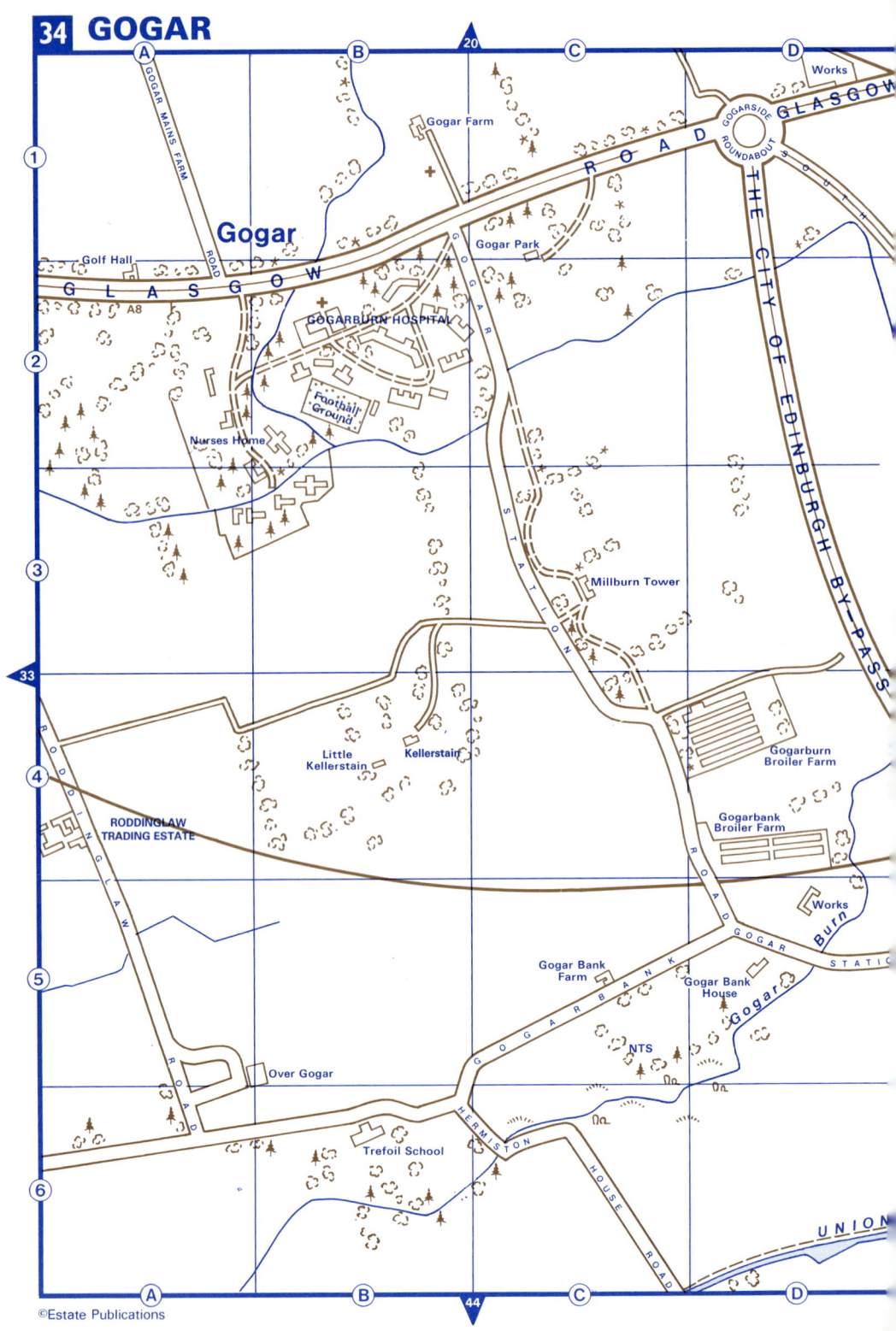

20

A B C D

Works

GOGARSIDE ROUNDABOUT

GLASGOW

THE CITY OF EDINBURGH BY-PASS

GOGAR MAINS FARM ROAD

1

Gogar Farm

Gogar

Golf Hall

GLASGOW ROAD

A8

Gogar Park

GOGAR ROAD

2

GOGARBURN HOSPITAL

Football Ground

Nurses Home

3

Millburn Tower

STATION ROAD

33

Little Kellerstain

Kellerstain

Gogarburn Broiler Farm

4

RODDINGLAW TRADING ESTATE

RODDINGLAW ROAD

Gogarbank Broiler Farm

Works

GOGAR STATION ROAD

Gogar Burn

5

Gogar Bank Farm

Gogar Bank House

GOGARBANK ROAD

NTS

Gogar Burn

STATIO

Over Gogar

HERMISTON HOUSE ROAD

6

Trefoil School

UNION

A B C D

44

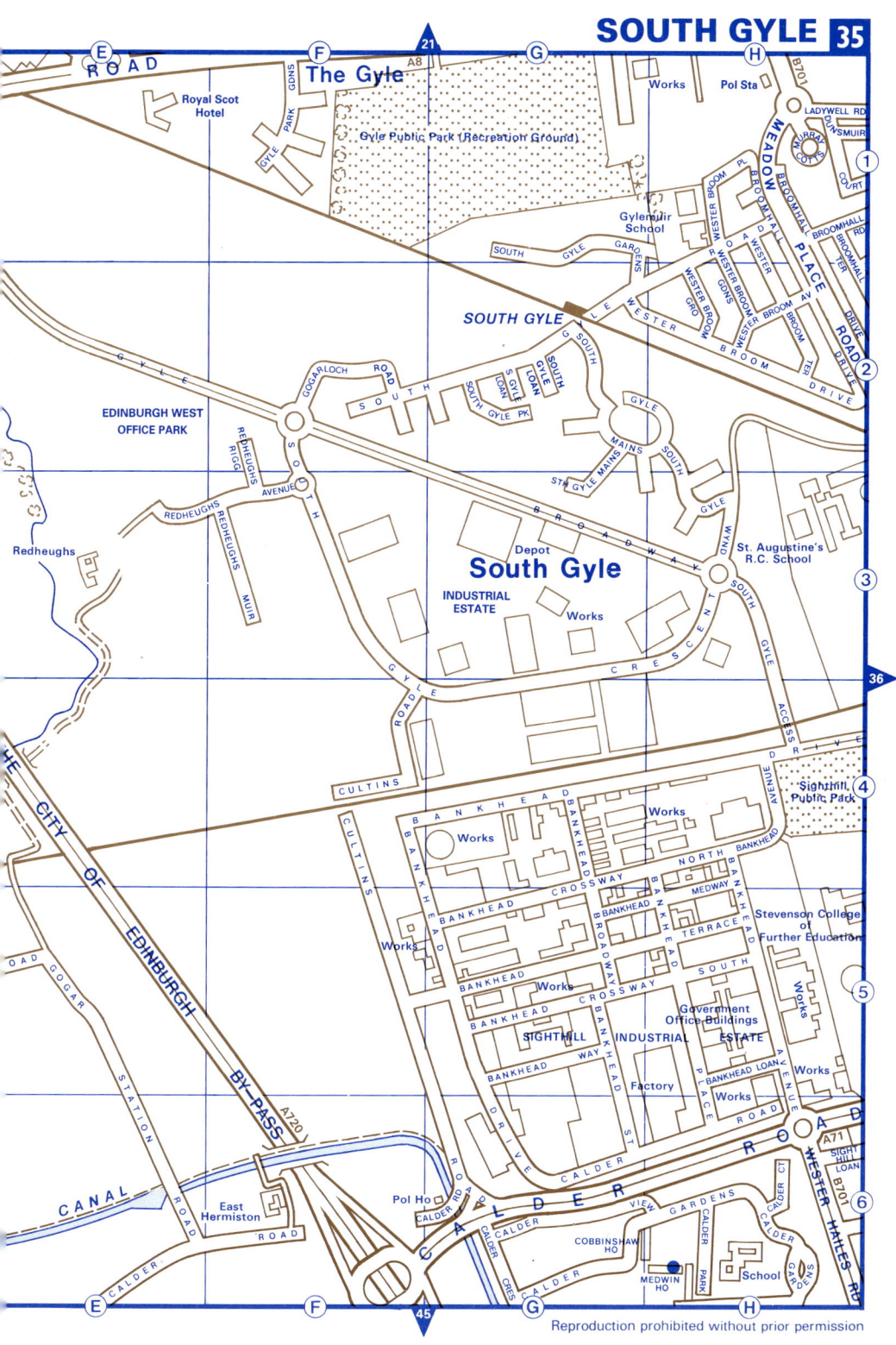

The Gyle

Royal Scot Hotel

Gyle Public Park (Recreation Ground)

Works Pol Sta

LADYWELL RD

Gylemuir School

SOUTH GYLE

EDINBURGH WEST OFFICE PARK

Redheughs

South Gyle
INDUSTRIAL ESTATE

Depot

Works

St. Augustine's R.C. School

BROADWAY

CULTINS

Sighthill Public Park

Works

BANKHEAD CROSSWAY

North Bankhead

MEDWAY

Stevenson College of Further Education

Works

Works

BANKHEAD CROSSWAY

Government Office Buildings

SIGHTHILL INDUSTRIAL ESTATE

Works

Factory

Works

CANAL

East Hermiston

Pol Ho

COBBINSHAW HO

MEDWIN HO

School

CITY OF EDINBURGH BY-PASS

A720

STATION ROAD

CALDER

CALDER ROAD

WESTER HAILES RD

A71

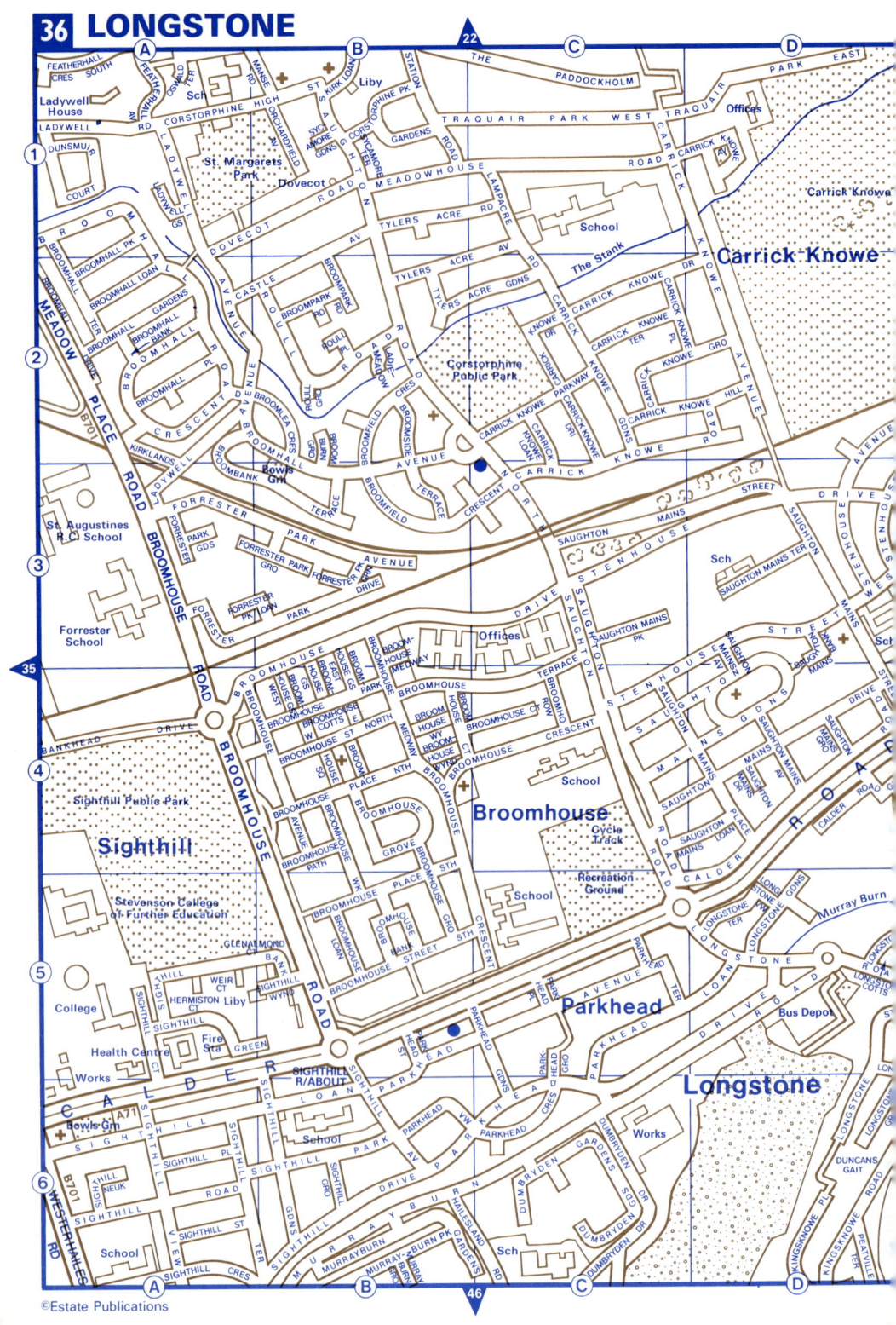

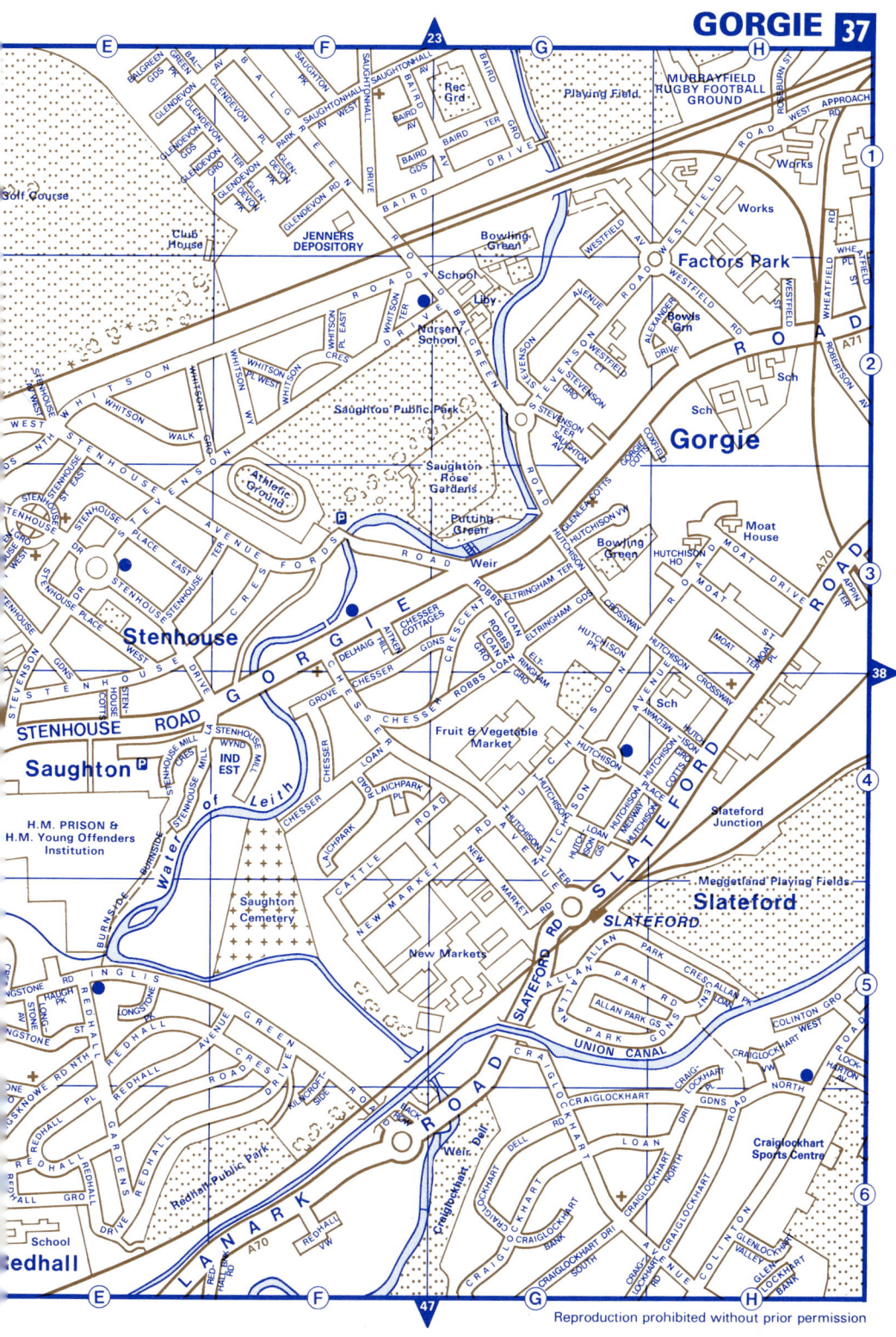

MURRAYFIELD RUGBY FOOTBALL GROUND

Golf Course

Club House

JENNERS DEPOSITORY

Bowling Green

School

Liby

Nursery School

Saughton Public Park

Factors Park

Gorgie

Works

Works

Bowls Grn

Sch

Sch

Athletic Ground

Saughton Rose Gardens

Putting Green

Weir

Bowling Green

Moat House

Stenhouse

Water of Leith

STENHOUSE ROAD

Saughton

Delhaig

Chesser

Chesser Cottages

Robbs Loan

Eltringham Ter

Glenlea Cotts

Hutchison Vw

Crossway

Hutchison Crossway

Moat

Hutchison

Fruit & Vegetable Market

Sch

H.M. PRISON & H.M. Young Offenders Institution

Saughton Cemetery

Cattle

New Market

Laichpark

Slateford Junction

Meggetland Playing Fields

Slateford

New Markets

Allan Park

Union Canal

Slateford

Craiglockhart Sports Centre

Redhall Public Park

Redhall

School

Weir

Craiglockhart

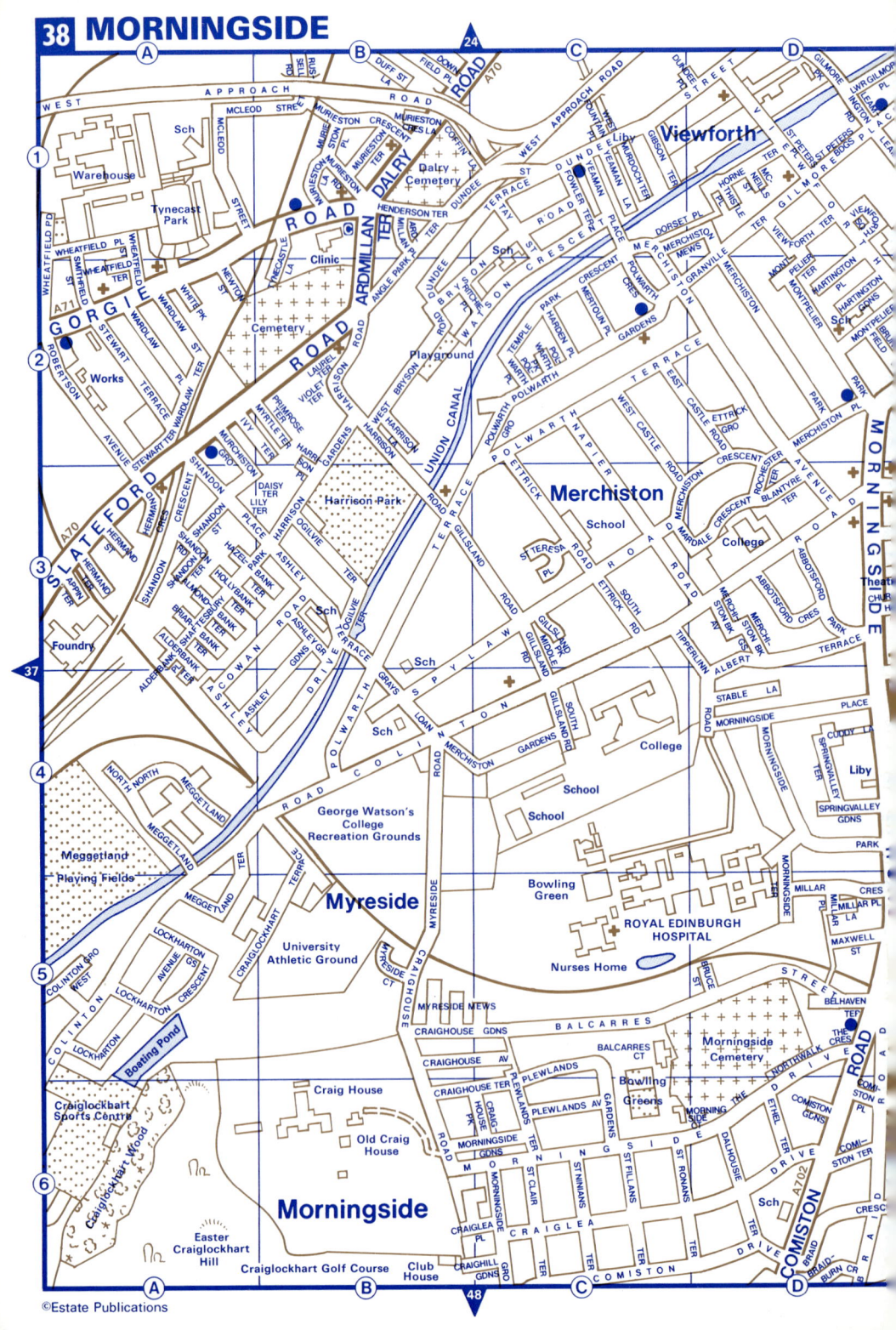

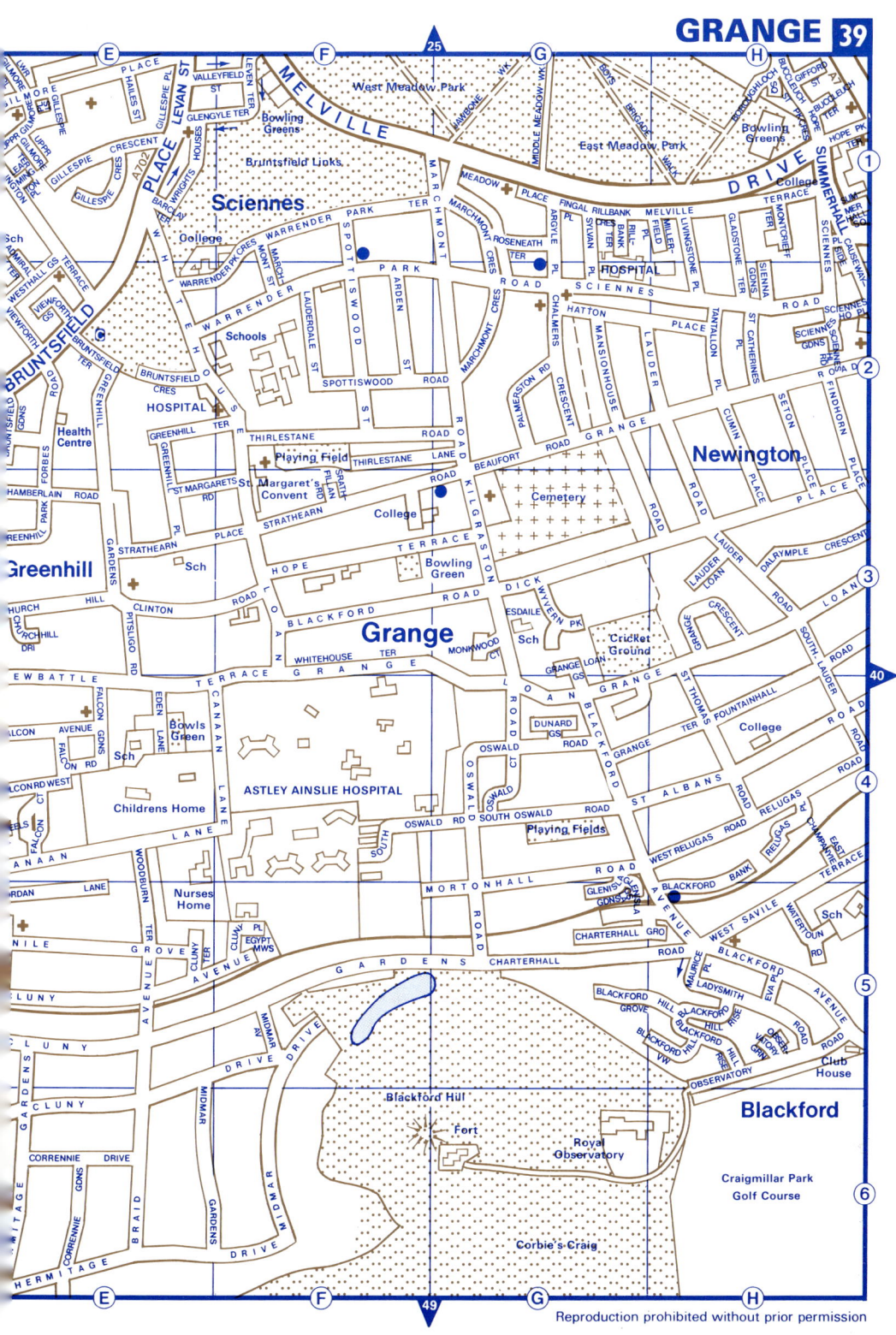

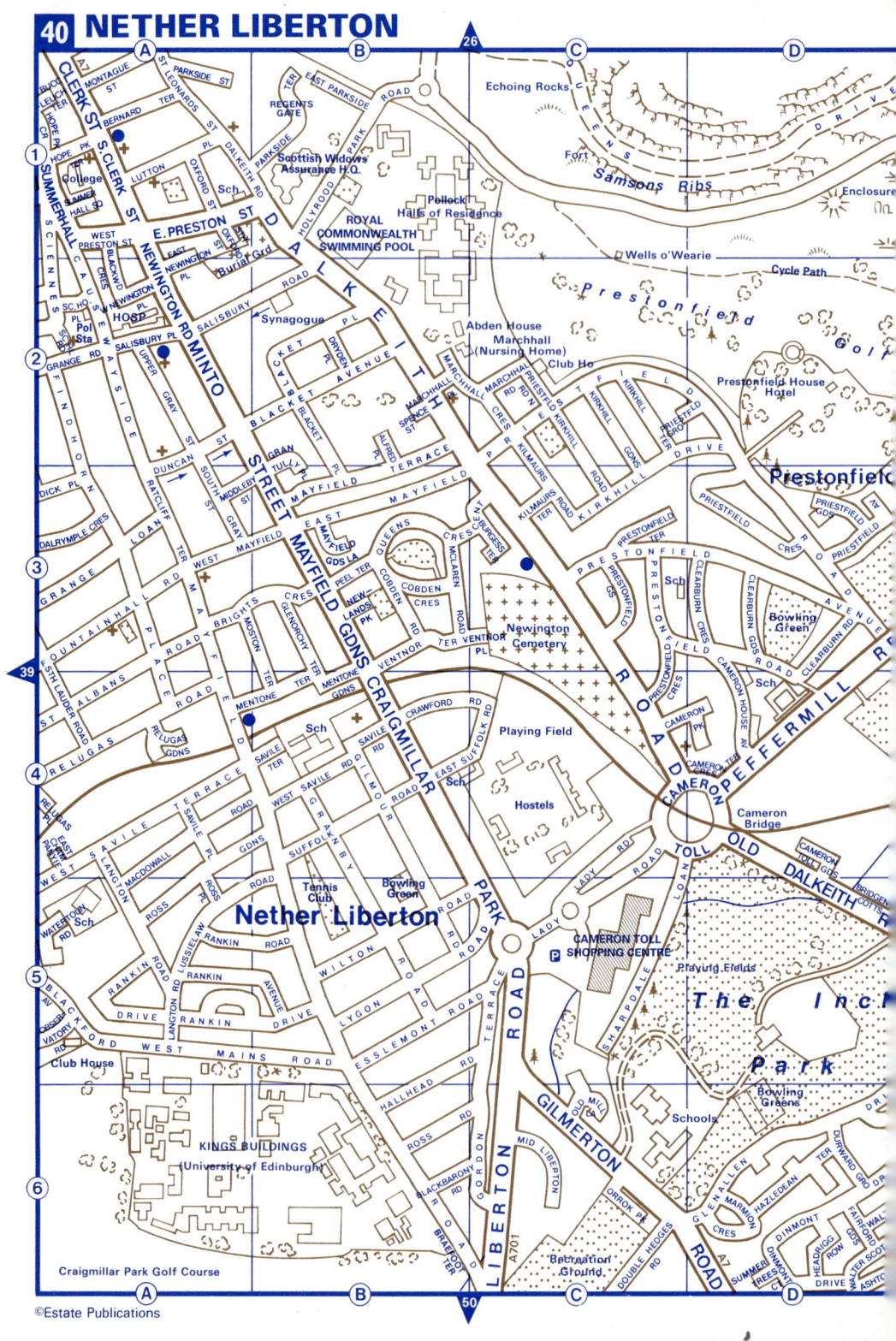

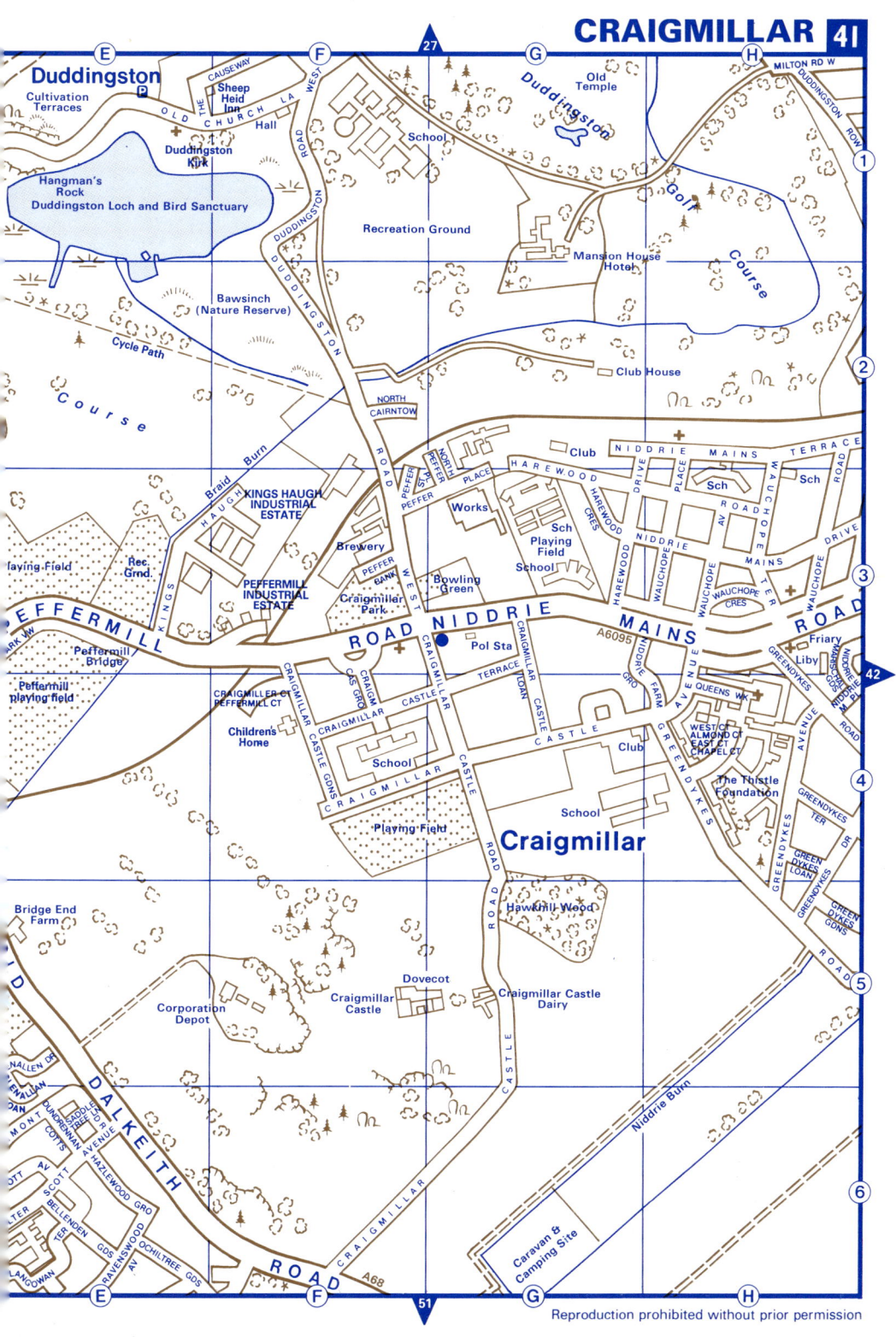

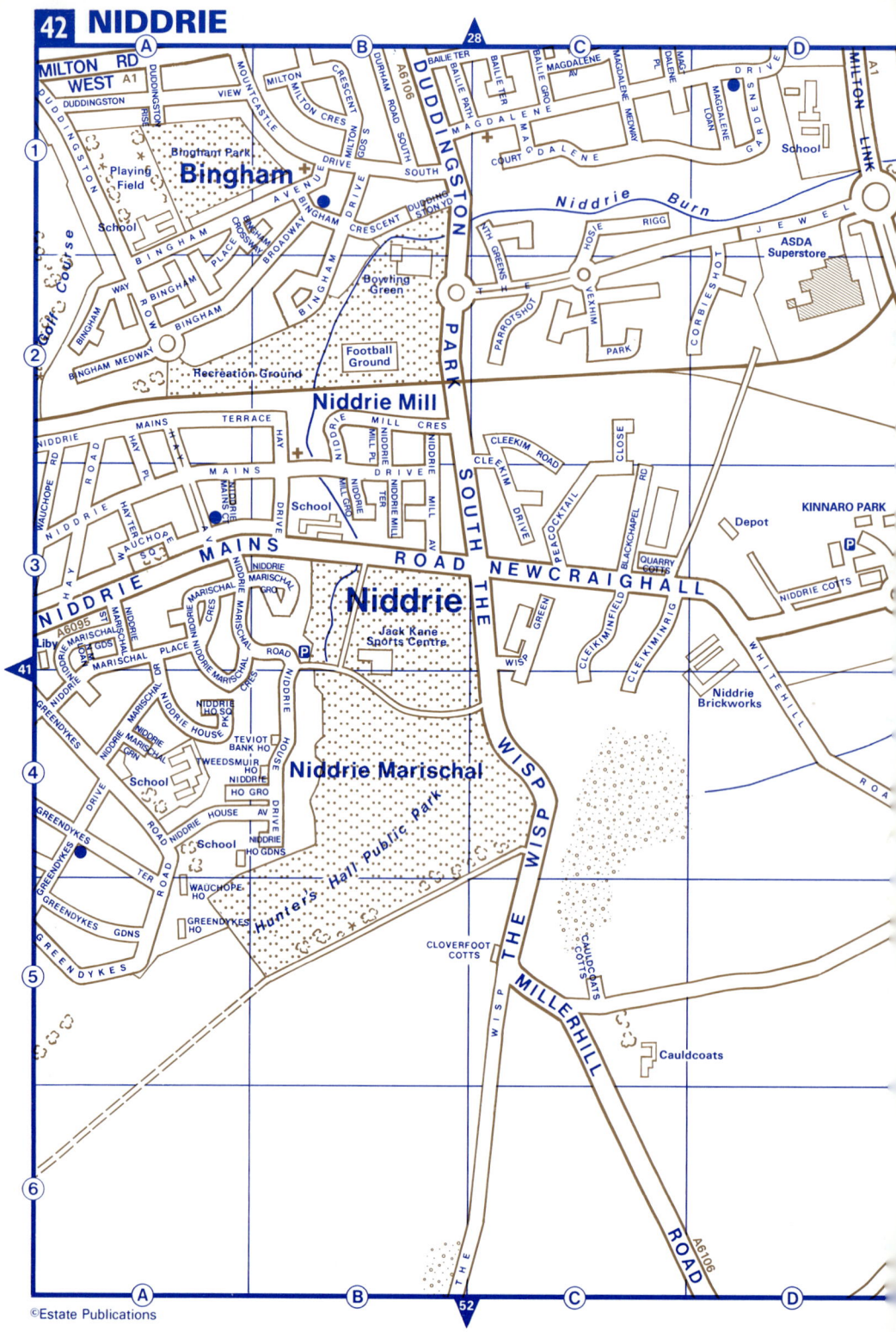

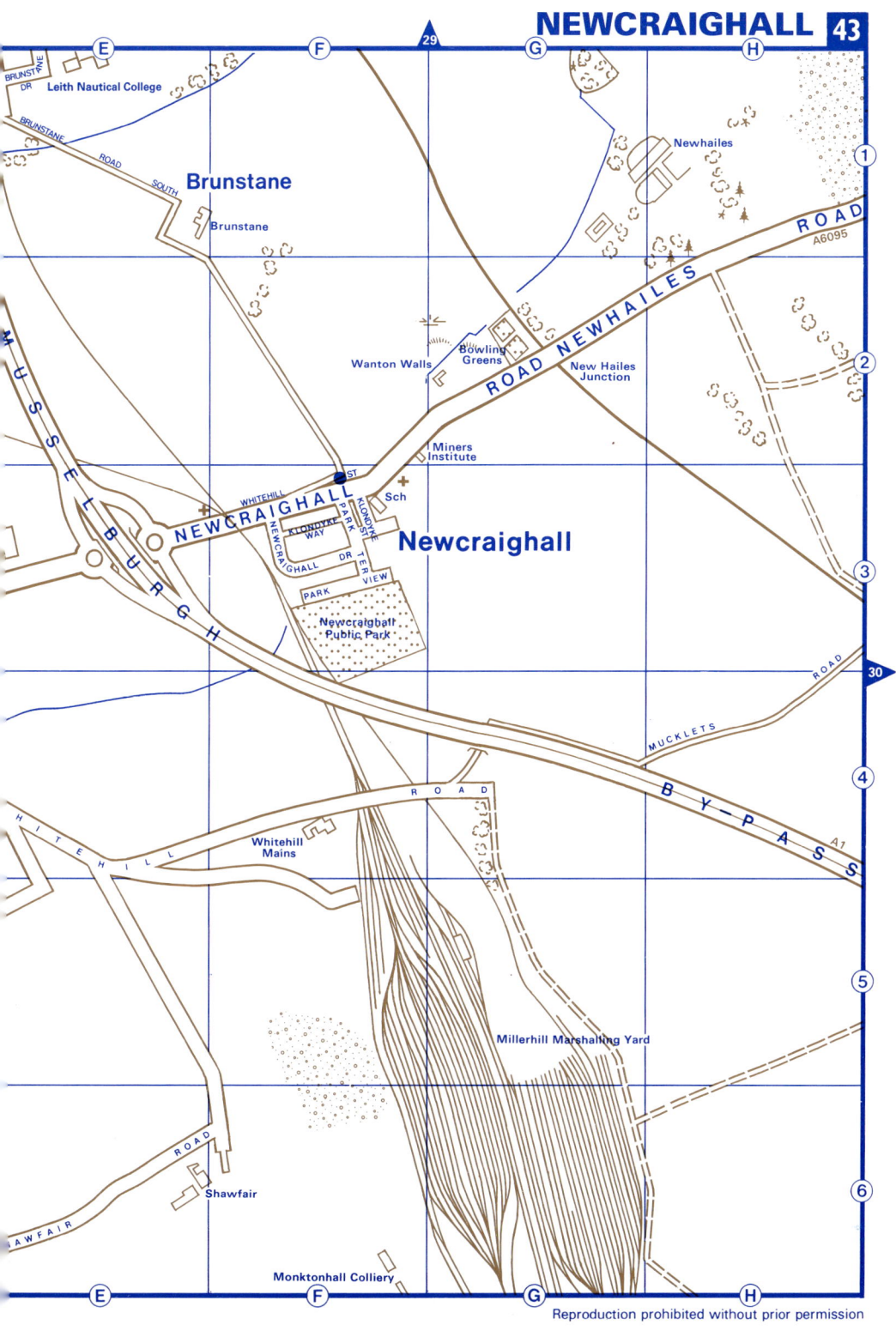

E · F · 29 · G · H

Leith Nautical College

BRUNSTANE DR

BRUNSTANE ROAD SOUTH

Brunstane

Brunstane

Newhailes

1

ROAD NEWHAILES ROAD A6095

Wanton Walls

Bowling Greens

New Hailes Junction

2

Miners Institute

WHITEHILL ST

NEWCRAIGHALL

NEWCRAIGHALL Sch

KLONDYKE WAY

KLONDYKE TER

PARK VIEW

PARK DR

Newcraighall

3

PARK

Newcraighall Public Park

MUSSELBURGH

ROAD

30

MUCKLETS

4

BY-PASS

A1

WHITEHILL

Whitehill Mains

ROAD

5

Millerhill Marshalling Yard

LAWFAIR ROAD

6

Shawfair

Monktonhall Colliery

E · F · G · H

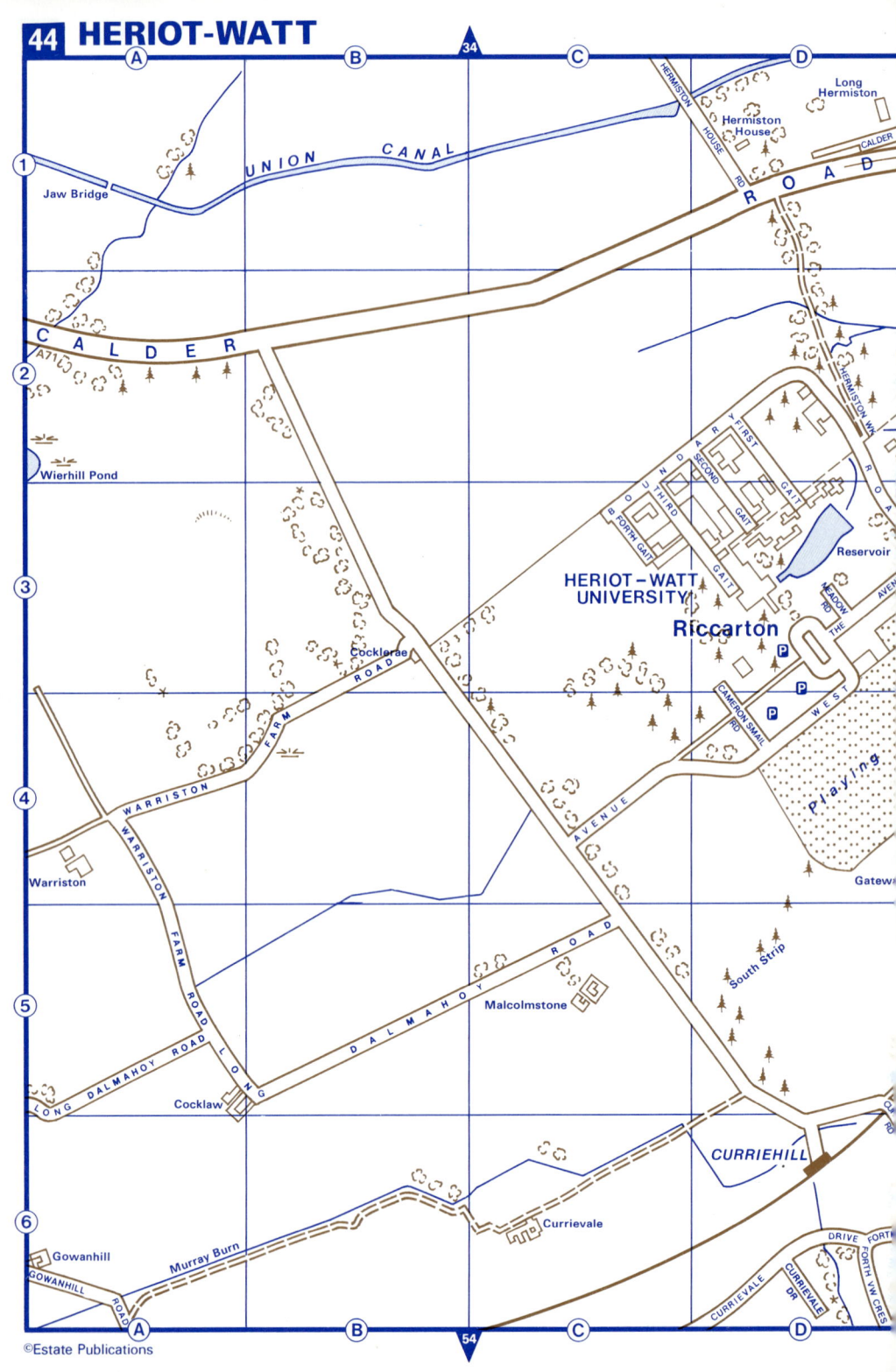

A   B   34   C   D

1

UNION CANAL

Jaw Bridge

Hermiston
Hermiston House
Hermiston House
Long Hermiston

CALDER ROAD

CALDER

A71

2

Wierhill Pond

FIRST GAIT
SECOND GAIT
THIRD GAIT
FORTH GAIT
BOUNDARY ROAD
HERMISTON WK
HERMISTON ROAD

Reservoir

3

HERIOT—WATT UNIVERSITY

Riccarton

MEADOW RD

THE AVENUE

Cocklerae

COCKLERAE ROAD

CAMERON SMAIL RD

P
P
P

WEST

WARRISTON FARM ROAD

Playing

4

Warriston

WARRISTON FARM ROAD

Gateway

South Strip

5

LONG DALMAHOY ROAD

DALMAHOY ROAD

Malcolmstone

AVENUE

Cocklaw

CURRIEHILL

6

Gowanhill

GOWANHILL ROAD

Murray Burn

Currievale

DRIVE FORT

FORTH VW CRES

CURRIEVALE DR

CURRIEVALE

A   B   54   C   D

©Estate Publications

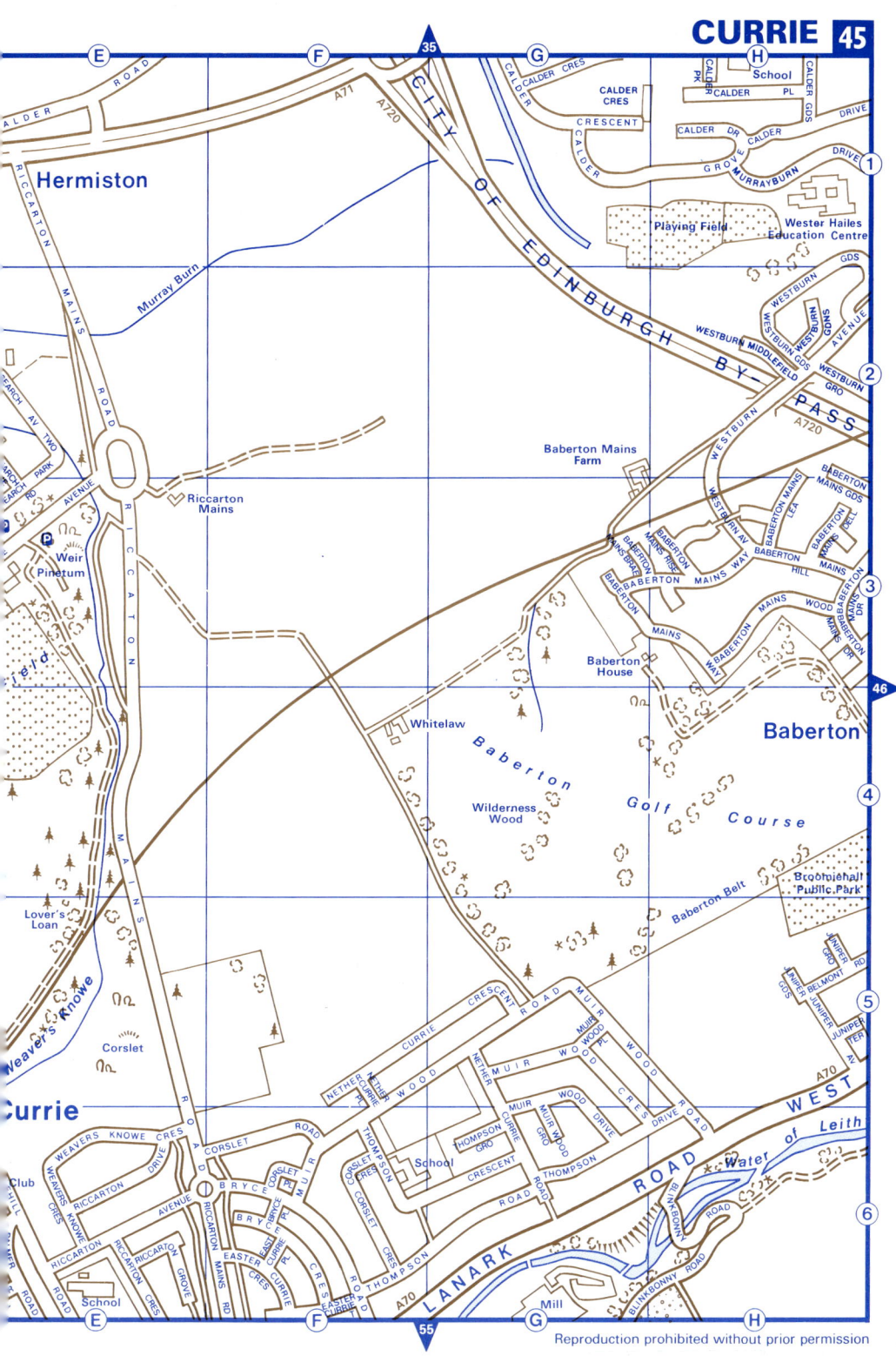

School

CALDER CRES

CALDER CRES

CALDER PL

CALDER GDS

CALDER DRIVE

CRESCENT

CALDER DR CALDER

CALDER GROVE

MURRAYBURN

DRIVE

Hermiston

A71

A720

CITY OF EDINBURGH BY-

Murray Burn

CALDER

Playing Field

Wester Hailes Education Centre

WESTBURN GDS

WESTBURN GRO

WESTBURN AVENUE

WESTBURN MIDDLEFIELD

WESTBURN GDS

WESTBURN

PASS

A720

Baberton Mains Farm

WESTBURN

RESEARCH AV TWO

RESEARCH PARK

RD

AVENUE

Riccarton Mains

WESTBURN AV

BABERTON MAINS BRAE

BABERTON MAINS RISE

BABERTON MAINS LEA

BABERTON MAINS

BABERTON MAINS GDS

BABERTON MAINS DELL

BABERTON MAINS

Weir Pinetum

RICCARTON

BABERTON

BABERTON MAINS WAY

BABERTON

HILL

BABERTON MAINS

BABERTON MAINS WOOD

BABERTON MAINS DR

MAINS

BABERTON MAINS WAY

Baberton House

46

Whitelaw

Baberton

MAINS

Baberton

Golf

Course

Wilderness Wood

Broomiehall Public Park

Lover's Loan

Baberton Belt

JUNIPER

BELMONT RD

JUNIPER GRO

JUNIPER CRES

Weavers Knowe

Corslet

JUNIPER BELMONT

JUNIPER

JUNIPER TER

A70

CRESCENT ROAD

MUIR WOOD

MUIR WOOD PL

MUIR WOOD CRES

MUIR WOOD DRIVE

MUIR WOOD ROAD

WEST

Water of Leith

Currie

WEAVERS KNOWE CRES

NETHER PL

NETHER CURRIE

CURRIE

WOOD

NETHER CURRIE

MUIR WOOD GRO

THOMPSON GRO

THOMPSON

CURRIE

CRESCENT

THOMPSON

ROAD

A70

ROAD

LANARK

ROAD

BLINKBONNY ROAD

Club

WEAVERS KNOWE CRES

RICCARTON

CORSLET DRIVE

ROAD

BRYCE AVENUE

CORSLET PL

BRYCE CRES

CORSLET CRES

THOMPSON

School

CRESCENT

Mill

BLINKBONNY ROAD

School

RICCARTON

RICCARTON CRES

AVENUE

RICCARTON MAINS RD

EASTER CURRIE CRES

EASTER CURRIE

THOMPSON ROAD

A70

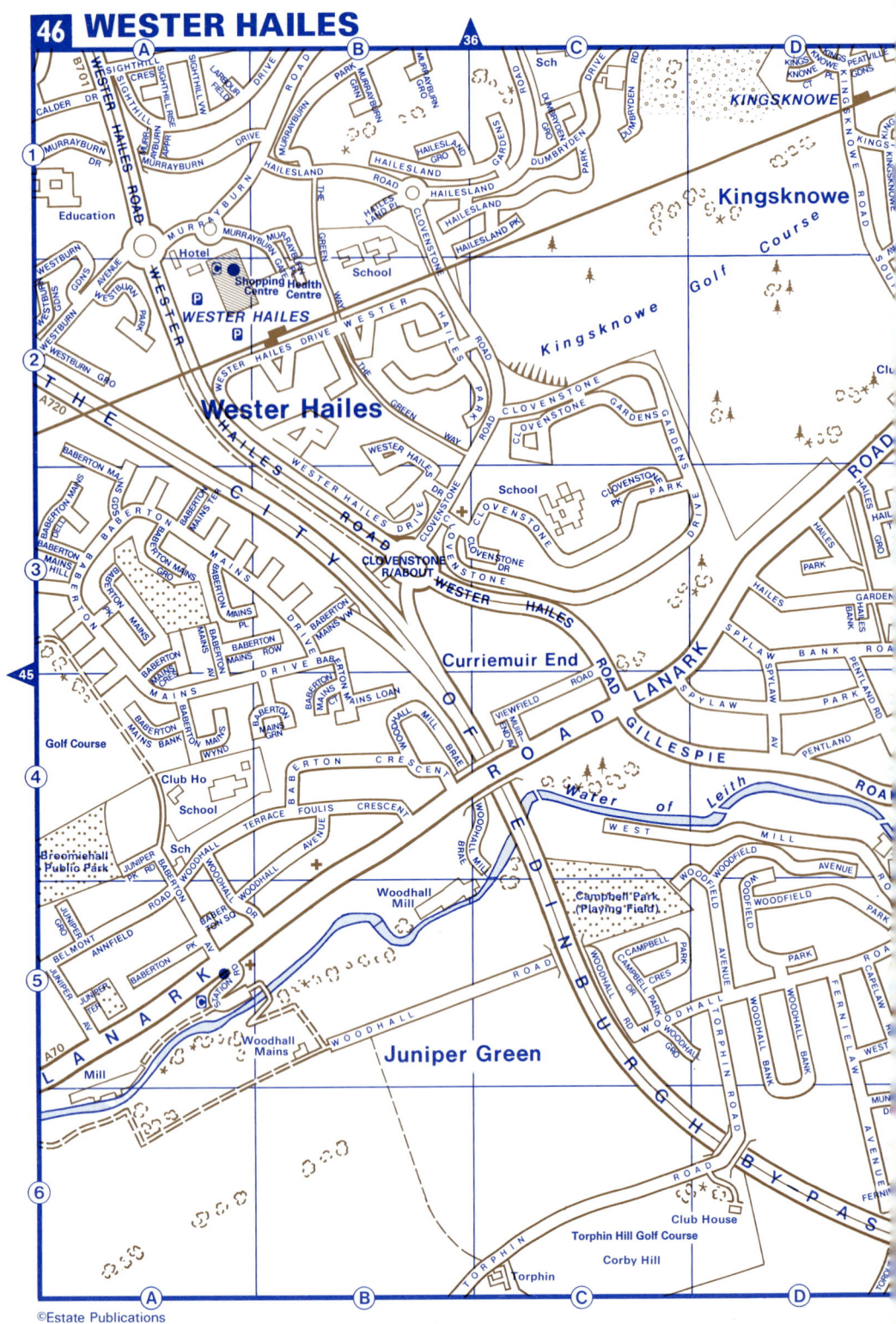

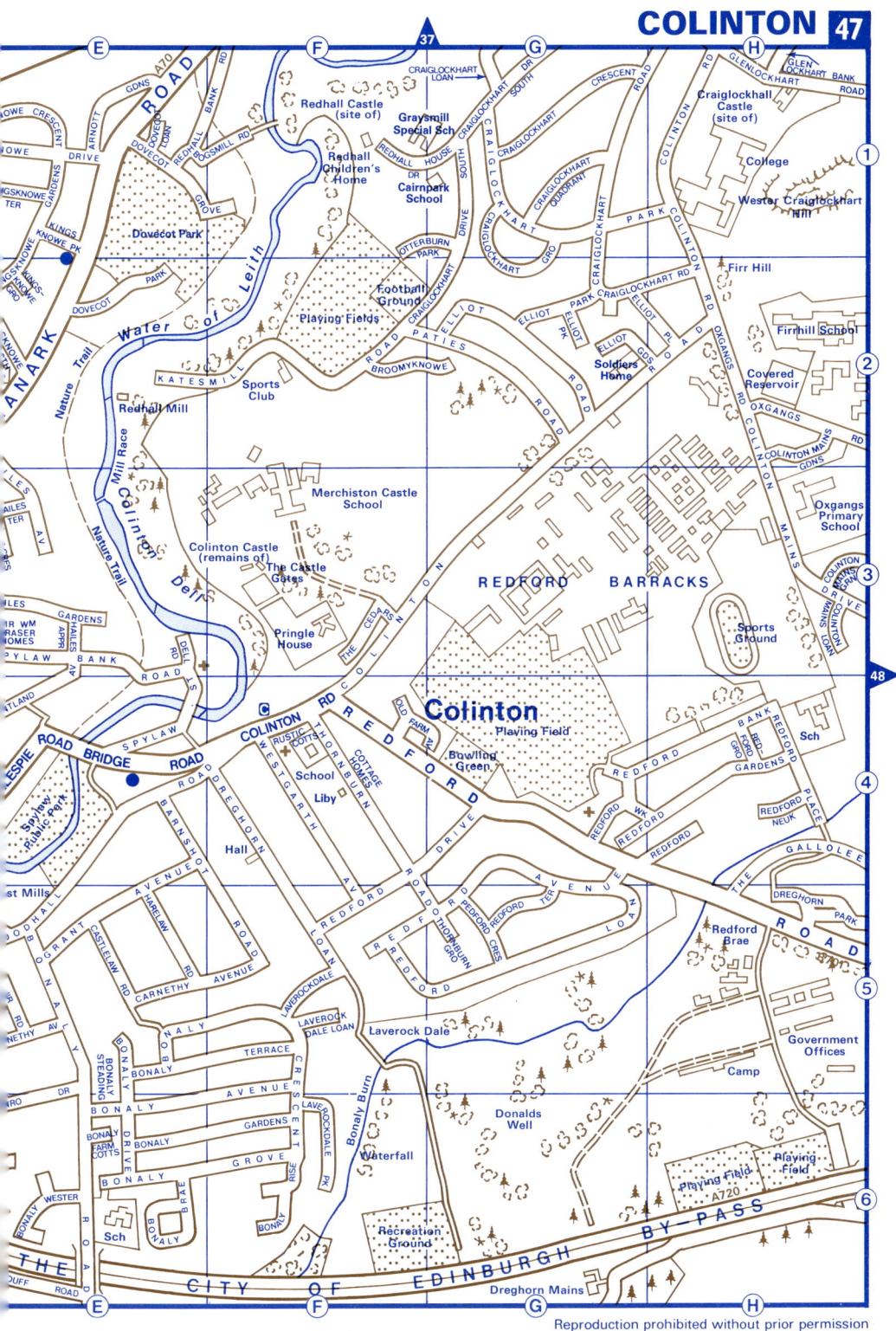

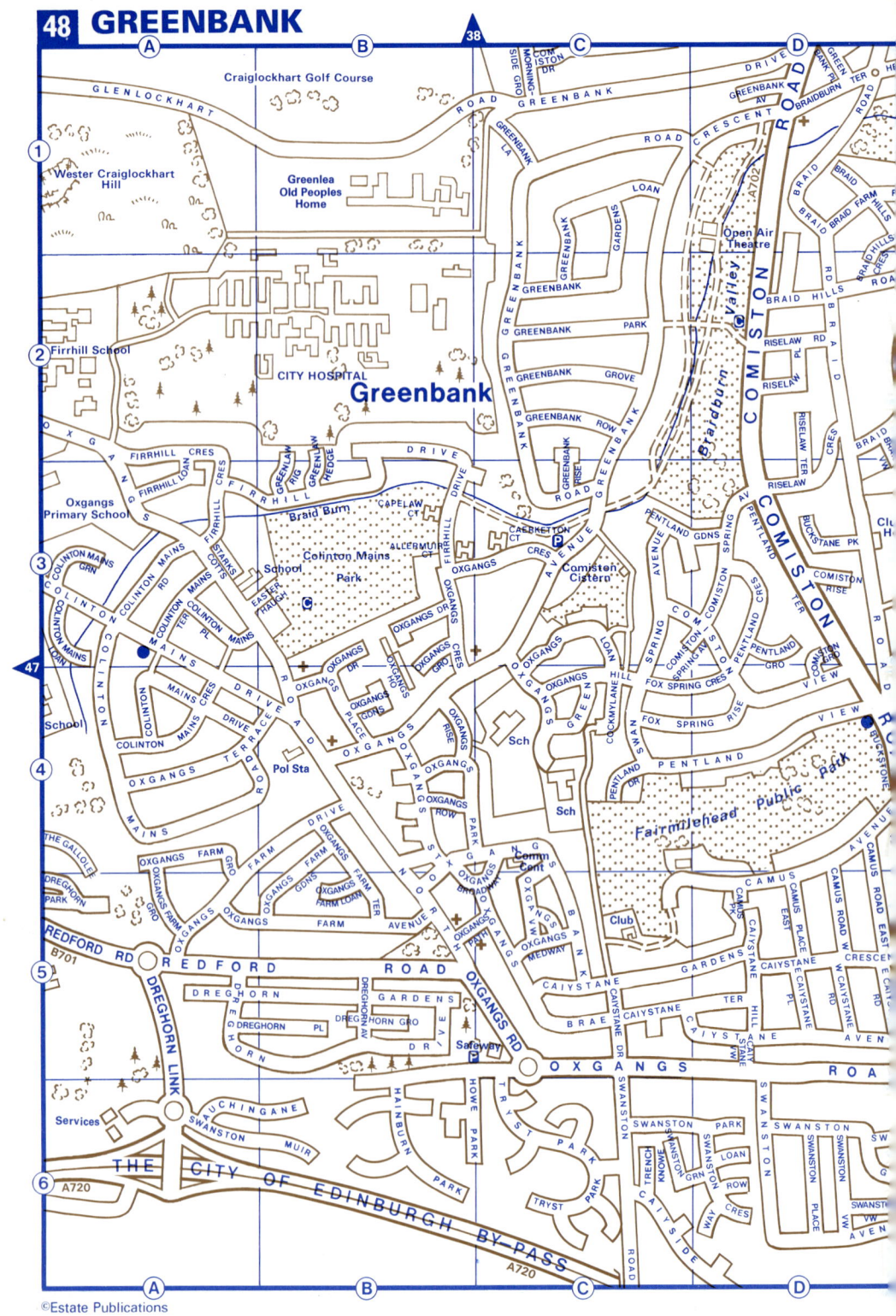

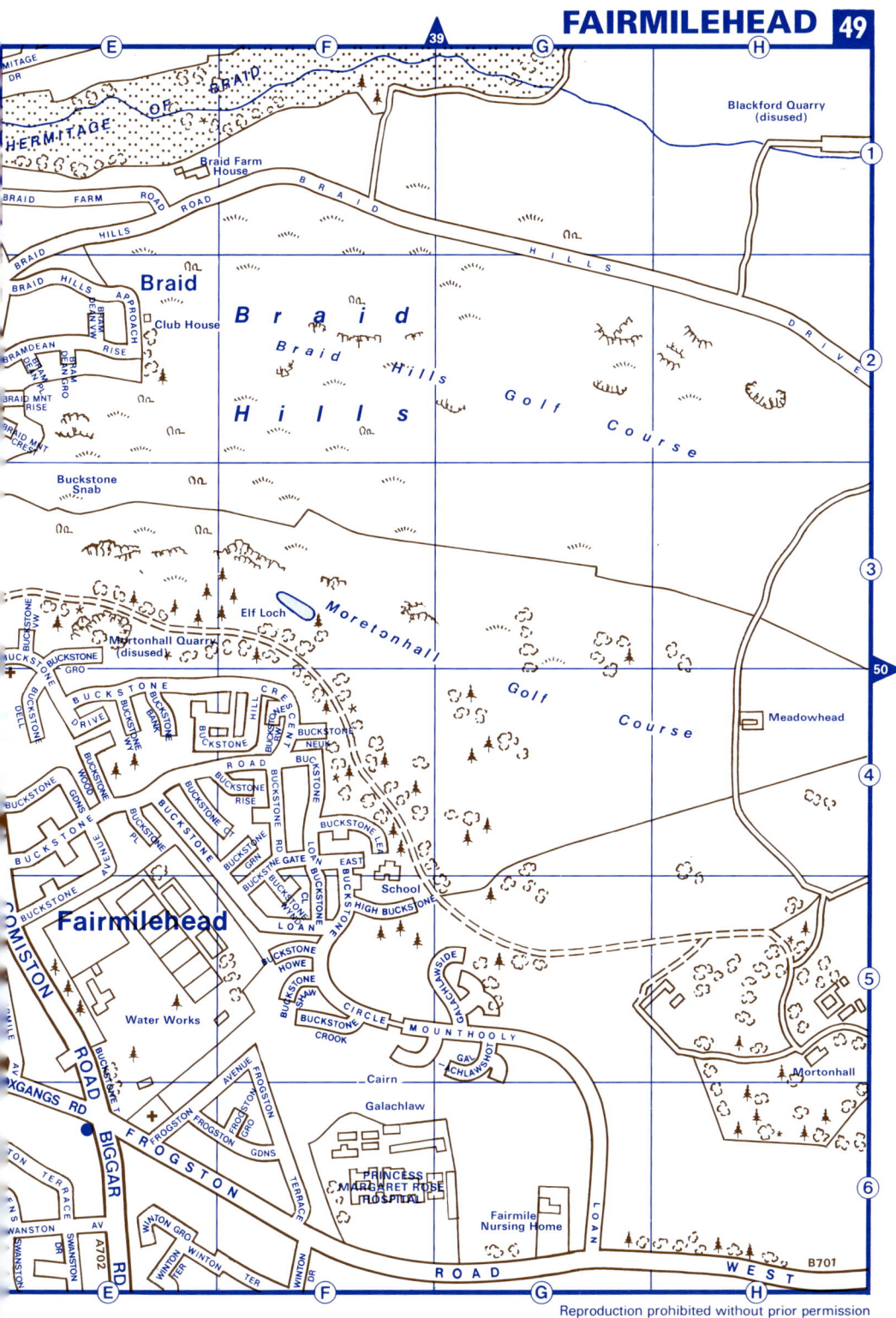

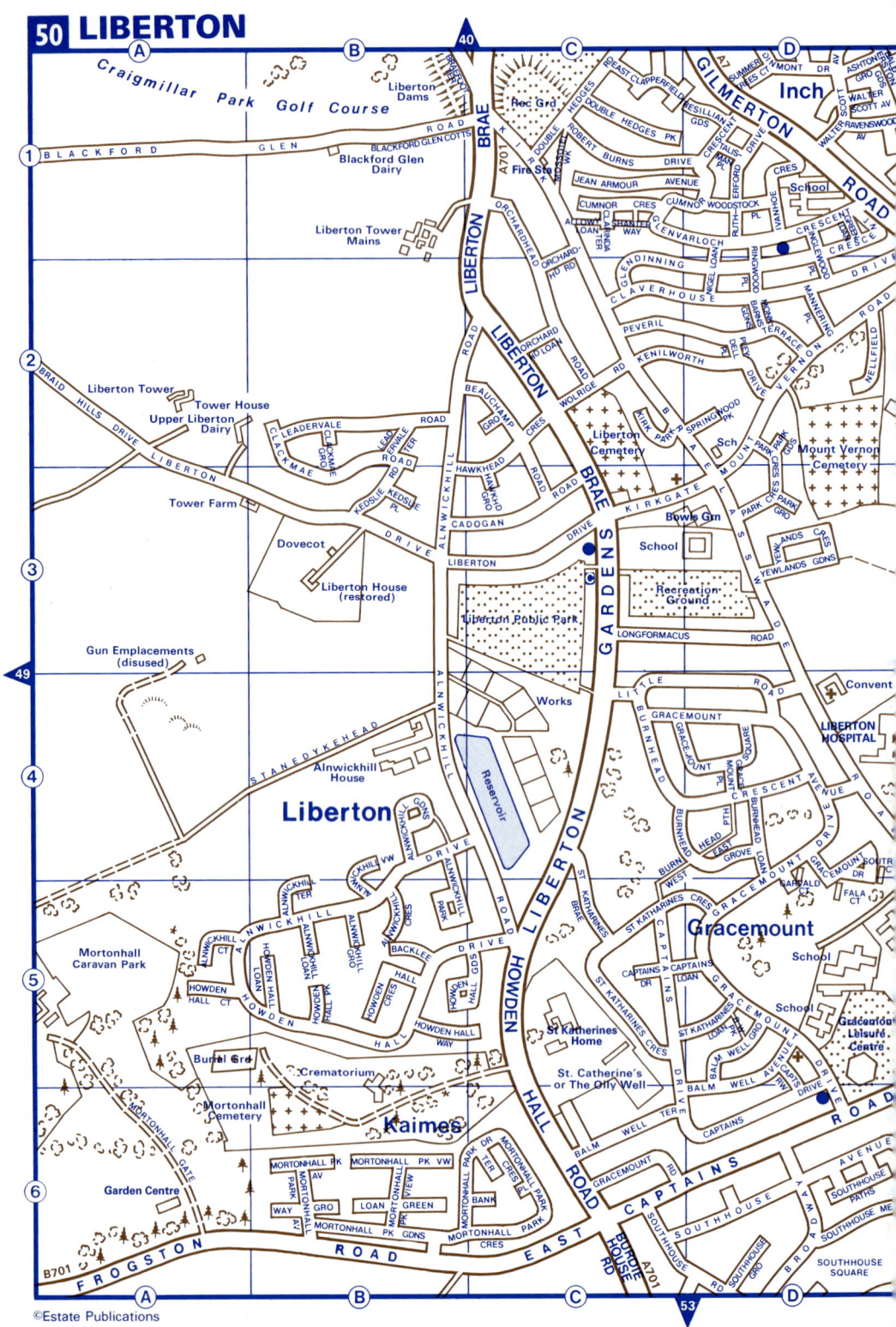

Craigmillar Park Golf Course

Liberton Dams

Rec Grd

GILMERTON

Inch

BLACKFORD GLEN
Blackford Glen Cotts
Blackford Glen Dairy

LIBERTON BRAE

A701

Fire Stn

EAST CLAPPERFIELD
DOUBLE HEDGES PK
DOUBLE HEDGES

ROBERT BURNS DRIVE

School

ROAD

Liberton Tower Mains

ORCHARDHEAD

ORCHARD RD RD

JEAN ARMOUR AVENUE

CUMNOR CRES
CUMNOR WOODSTOCK

ALLOWAY

GLENVARLOCH

IVANHOE

CRES

CRES

Liberton Tower

Tower House
Upper Liberton Dairy

LEADERVALE ROAD

CLACKMAE

LEADERVALE ROAD

KEDSLIE KEDSLIE PL

DRIVE

ORCHARD RD LOAN

BEAUCHAMP GRO

CRES

HAWKHEAD

ALNWICKHILL

CADOGAN

KENILWORTH

GLENDINNING

CLAVERHOUSE

PEVERIL

KIRK PARK

SPRINGWOOD

MOUNT

VERNON

Mount Vernon Cemetery

Tower Farm

Dovecot

Liberton House
(restored)

LIBERTON

DRIVE

Liberton Cemetery

KIRKGATE

Bowls Grn

School

Recreation Ground

PARK

YEWLANDS

YEWLANDS GDNS

Gun Emplacements
(disused)

49

ALNWICKHILL

Liberton Public Park

Reservoir

LONGFORMACUS ROAD

LITTLE

Works

GRACEMOUNT

BURNHEAD

GRACEMOUNT

BURNHEAD HEAD

ROAD

Convent

LIBERTON HOSPITAL

STANEDYKEHEAD

Alnwickhill House

Liberton

ALNWICKHILL
DRIVE

ALNWICKHILL GDNS

LIBERTON GARDENS

ST KATHARINES

BRAE

CRESCENT

AVENUE

BURN HEAD GROVE

EAST LOAN

WEST

GRACEMOUNT

AVENUE

GARFALD

FALA CT

SOUTR CT

Mortonhall Caravan Park

ALNWICKHILL TER
ALNWICKHILL CT

ALNWICKHILL LOAN

ALNWICKHILL CRES

HOWDEN HALL PK

ALNWICKHILL VW

ALNWICKHILL GRO

ALNWICKHILL PARK

BACKLEE

HOWDEN

HALL

HOWDEN HALL GDNS

DRIVE

HOWDEN HALL WAY

HOWDEN CRES

St Katherines Home

ST KATHARINES CRES

ST KATHARINES LOAN

Captains
CAPTAINS DR

Captains
LOAN

GRACEMOUNT

GRACEMOUNT DRIVE

Gracemount

School

School

Gracemount Leisure Centre

ROAD

Burial Grd

Crematorium

Mortonhall Cemetery

Kaimes

St Katherines
Home

St. Catherine's
or The Oily Well

BALM WELL GRO

BALM WELL TER

BALM WELL AVENUE

CAPTAINS

Garden Centre

MORTONHALL GATE

MORTONHALL PK
AV
WAY
GRO
AV

MORTONHALL PK VW
MORTONHALL
PARK
LOAN GREEN

MORTONHALL PK GDNS

MORTONHALL PARK DR
TER
CRES
BANK

MORTONHALL
PARK
VIEW

MORTONHALL PARK CRES

GRACEMOUNT

SOUTHHOUSE

BURDIE HOUSE RD

AVENUE

SOUTHHOUSE
PATHS

BROADWAY

SOUTHHOUSE
SQUARE

B701

FROGSTON ROAD

EAST CAPTAINS

A701

SOUTHHOUSE

SOUTHHOUSE SQUARE

GILMERTON 51

Edmonstone

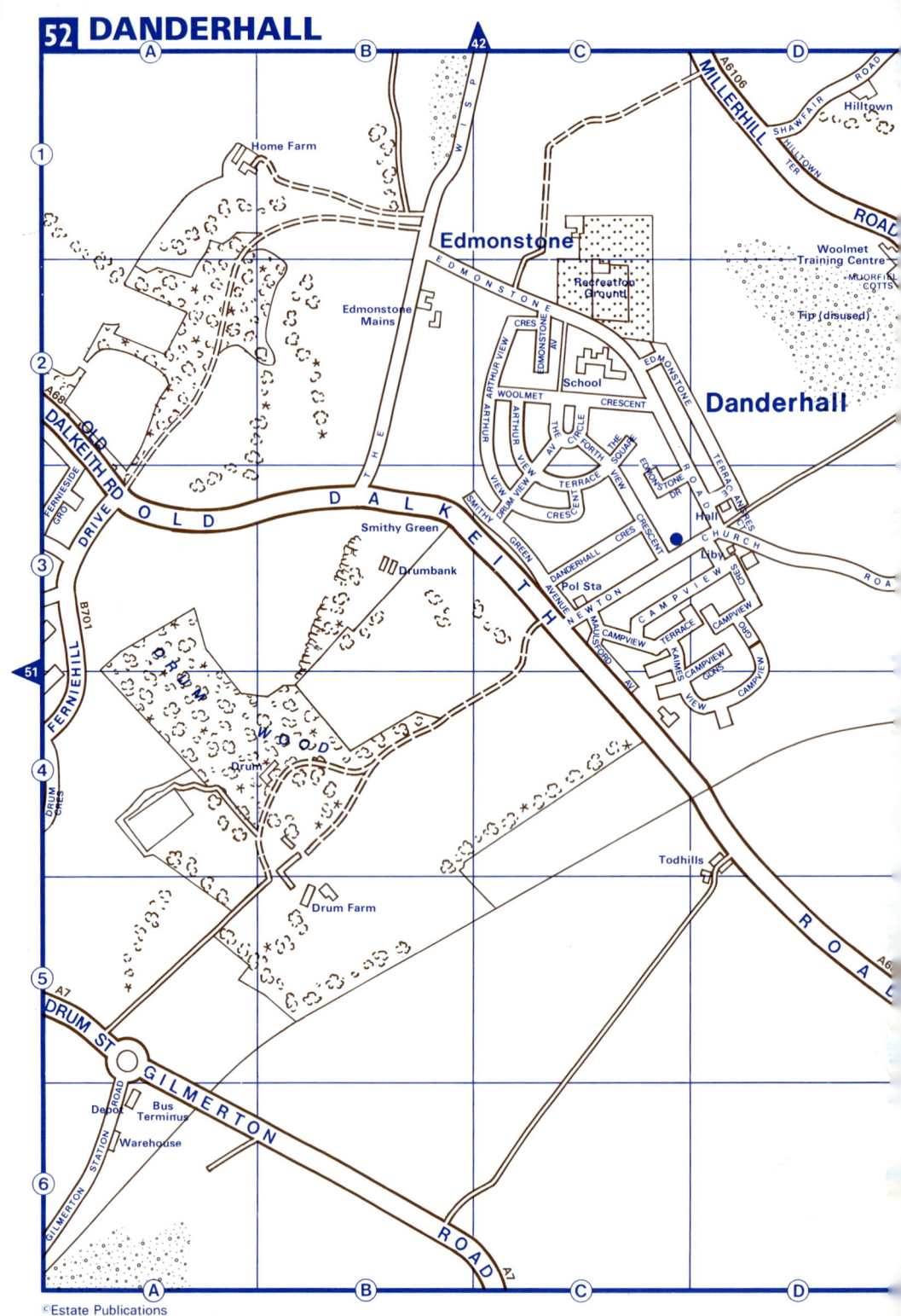

Home Farm

Edmonstone

Edmonstone Mains

Recreation Ground

Woolmet Training Centre

MUORFIN COTTS

Tip (disused)

School

Danderhall

Hilltown

SHAWFAIR

MILLERHILL

A6106

ROAD

A68

OLD DALKEITH RD

DALKEITH

DRIVE

FERNIESIDE GRO

FERNIEHILL

B701

OLD

DALKEITH

THE WISP

42

EDMONSTONE

CRES

EDMONSTONE

AV

EDMONSTONE

CRESCENT

WOOLMET

ARTHUR VIEW

ARTHUR

VIEW

ARTHUR VIEW DR

THE CYCLE

FORTH VIEW

THE SQUARE

EDMONSTONE DR

ROAD

TERRACE

AMBROSE

CHURCH

ROAD

TERRACE

CRESC

Hall

Lby

Smithy Green

Drumbank

DRUM

WOOD

Drum

Drum Farm

Smithy Green

DANDERHALL

AVENUE

NEWTON

Pol Sta

MALLISFORD

CAMPVIEW

AV

CAMPVIEW

TERRACE

KAIMES

VIEW

CAMPVIEW

GDNS

CAMPVIEW

CRES

CAMPVIEW

CRESCENT

NEWTON

CRES

Todhills

ROAD

A6

DRUM ST

A7

GILMERTON

Depot

Bus Terminus

Warehouse

GILMERTON STATION ROAD

ROAD

A7

51

© Estate Publications

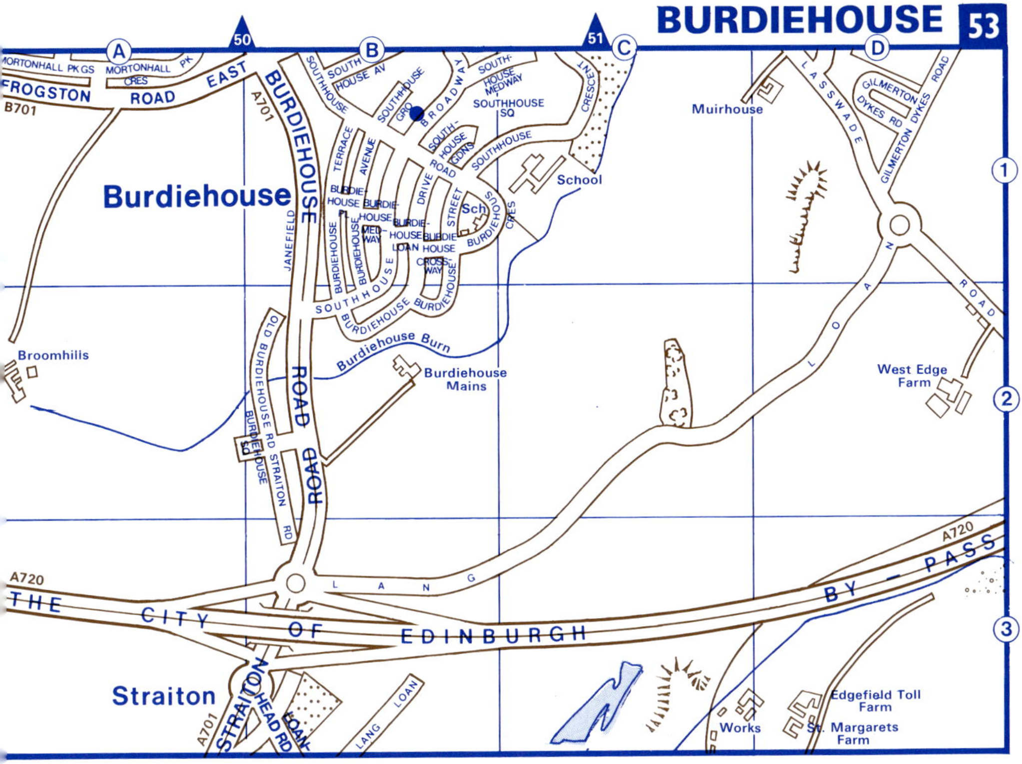

50 51

A B C D

1
2
3

MORTONHALL PK GS
MORTONHALL PK
FROGSTON ROAD EAST
B701

SOUTH HOUSE AV
SOUTHHOUSE
SOUTH HOUSE TERRACE
BROADWAY
SOUTH HOUSE ROAD
SOUTHHOUSE STREET
SOUTHHOUSE SQ
SOUTH- HOUSE MEDWAY
SOUTHHOUSE CRESCENT
Muirhouse

Burdiehouse

BURDIEHOUSE ROAD
A701
JANEFIELD
BURDIEHOUSE AVENUE
BURDIEHOUSE TERRACE
SOUTHHOUSE CRES
BURDIE- HOUSE
BURDIE- HOUSE MED- WAY
BURDIE HOUSE LOAN HOUSE
BURDIEHOUSE CROSS WAY
BURDIEHOUSE
Sch
School

GILMERTON DYKES RD
GILMERTON DYKES ROAD
LASSWADE ROAD

Broomhills

OLD BURDIEHOUSE RD STRAITON
BURDIEHOUSE ROAD

Burdiehouse Burn
Burdiehouse Mains

West Edge Farm

LOAN ROAD

A720
A720

THE CITY OF EDINBURGH BY - PASS
LANG LOAN

Straiton

STRAITON HEAD RD
A701
LANG LOAN

Edgefield Toll Farm
Works
St. Margarets Farm

A B C D

4
5
6

57

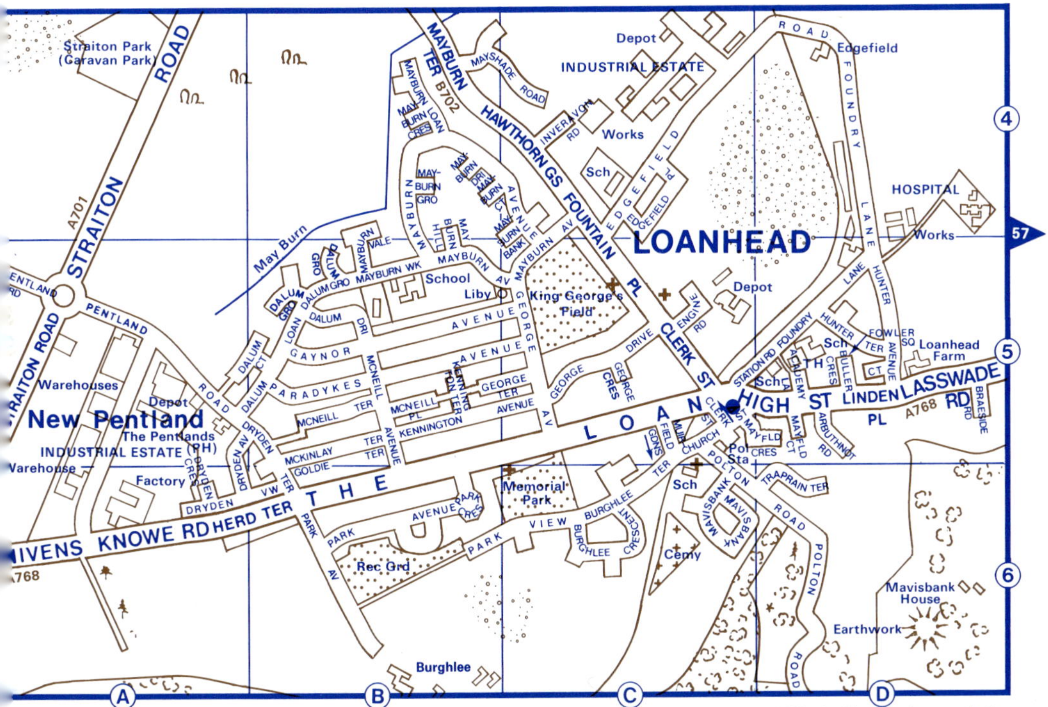

Straiton Park (Caravan Park)

STRAITON ROAD
A701

MAYBURN TERRACE B702
MAYBURN CRES
MAYSHADE ROAD
INVERION RD
Depot
Edgefield
INDUSTRIAL ESTATE

ROAD
FOUNDRY LANE

HAWTHORN GS
FOUNTAIN PL
Works
Sch
EDGEFIELD

May Burn
MAYBURN GRO
MAY- BURN LOAN
MAY- BURN VALE
MAYBURN WK
MAY- BURN AVEN
MAYBURN BANK
MAYBURN AV

LOANHEAD

HOSPITAL
Works

School
Liby
King George's Field
Depot

DALUM LOAN
DALUM GRO
DALUM
DALUM
GAYNOR
PARADYKES
MCNEILL
MCNEILL
MCNEILL PL
MCNEILL TER
MCKINLAY TER
GOLDIE
DRYDEN TER
DRYDEN AV
DRYDEN

GEORGE DRIVE
GEORGE AVENUE
AVENUE
AVENUE
KENNINGTON AVENUE
KENNINGTON PL
GEORGE TER

CLERK ST
THE LOAN
ENGINE RD
Church
POLTON
Pol Sta

STATION RD
FOUNDRY
HUNTER
HUNTER AVENUE
FOWLER TER
BURDIE
Sch
Sch
Loanhead Farm
Depot

A768
HIGH ST
LINDEN LASSWADE RD
PL
BRAESIDE
ARBUTHNOT RD
MAYFIELD
TRAPRAIN TER

PENTLAND ROAD
PENTLAND
Warehouses
Depot
Factory
New Pentland
The Pentlands
INDUSTRIAL ESTATE (PH)
Varehouse

NIVENS KNOWE RD
HERD TER
THE
PARK AV
PARK
AVENUE
BURGHLEE
VIEW
BURGHLEE CRES
Memorial Park
Rec Grd
Cemy
MAVISBANK
MAVISBANK
POLTON RD
POLTON TER

Mavisbank House
Earthwork

Burghlee

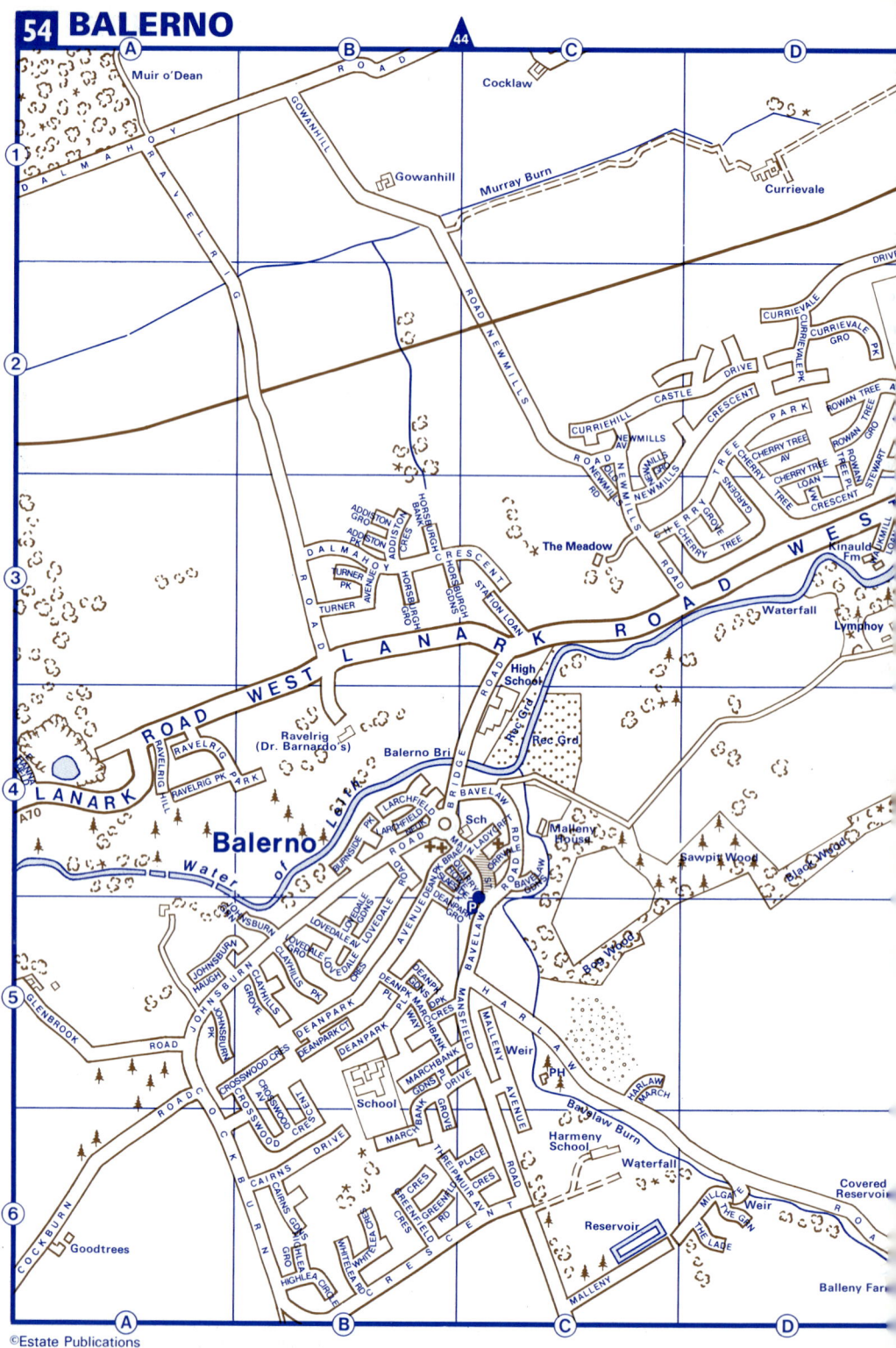

44

A   B   C   D

1

2

3

4

5

6

Muir o'Dean

Cocklaw

Gowanhill

Murray Burn

Currievale

DALMAHOY   ROAD   RAVELRIG

GOWANHILL

ROAD   NEWMILLS   PK

CURRIEVALE GRO
CURRIEVALE PK
CURRIEVALE GRO
CASTLE   DRIVE
CRESCENT
PARK
ROWAN TREE AV
CURRIEHILL
NEWMILLS AV
ROWAN TREE GRO
ROWAN TREE PK
STEWART
NEWMILLS ROAD
NEWMILLS RO
NEWMILLS
CHERRY TREE AV
CHERRY TREE LOAN
CHERRY TREE CRESCENT
CARRONS
CHERRY TREE
T REE   CHERRY   Y GROVE   R R

The Meadow

Kinauld Fm
Waterfall
Lymphoy

ADDISTON GRO
ADDISTON PK
ADDISTON CRES
DALMAHOY ROAD
TURNER PK
TURNER AVENUE
TURNER
HORSBURGH BANK
HORSBURGH GDNS
HORSBURGH
CRESCENT
STATION LOAN

LANARK   ROAD   WEST
WEST   LANARK   ROAD

High School

ROAD

BRIDGE ROAD

Ravelrig
(Dr. Barnardo's)
Balerno Bri

Rec Grd

RAVELRIG HILL
RAVELRIG PK
RAVELRIG PARK

LANARK
A70

Balerno

Water   of   Leith

BAVELAW

Malleny House

Sawpit Wood

Black Wood

BURNSIDE PK
LARCHFIELD
ARNFIELD
Sch
ST JOSEPHS
OUR LADYS RC
MARY
BAVELAW
BAVELAW ROAD

P

Bog Wood

JOHNSBURN HAUGH
JOHNSBURN ROAD
JOHNSBURN PK
CLAYHILLS GROVE
CLAYHILLS
LOVEDALE AV
LOVEDALE GDNS
LOVEDALE CRES
LOVEDALE PK
LOVEDALE
AVENUE DEANPARK BRAE
DEANPARK GRO
DEANPARK
DEANPK PL
DEANPK PLWAY
DEANPARK CT
MARCHBANK PL
MARCHBANK CRES
DPK
MANSFIELD ROAD
MALLENY AVENUE
HARLAW ROAD

Weir

Glenbrook

CROSSWOOD CRES
CROSSWOOD
CROSSWOOD CRESCENT
CAIRNS GDNS
CAIRNS GRO
DEANPARK DRIVE
School
MARCHBANK GDNS
MARCHBANK GROVE
MARCHBANK
THREEMILE
GREENFIELD PLACE
GREENFIELD CRES
GREENFIELD
CRES
PH
Weir
HARLAW MARCH
Bavelaw Burn
Harmeny School
Waterfall
MILLGATE
THE GLEN
Weir
Covered Reservoir

COCKBURN
Goodtrees
HIGHLEA GRO
HIGHLEA CIRCLE
WHITELAW RO
CREE
WHITELAW
Reservoir
THE LADE
MALLENY
Balleny Far

A   B   C   D

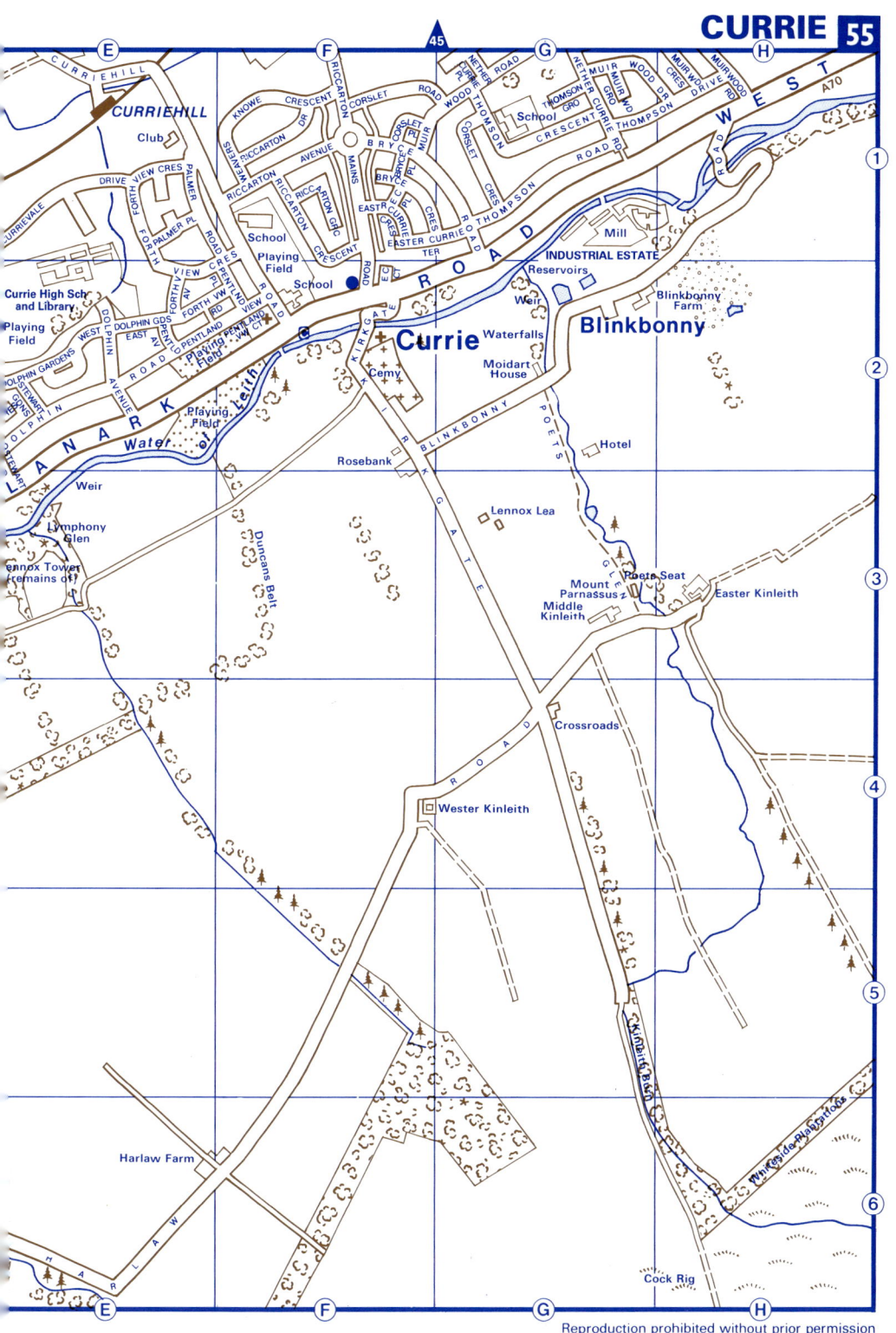

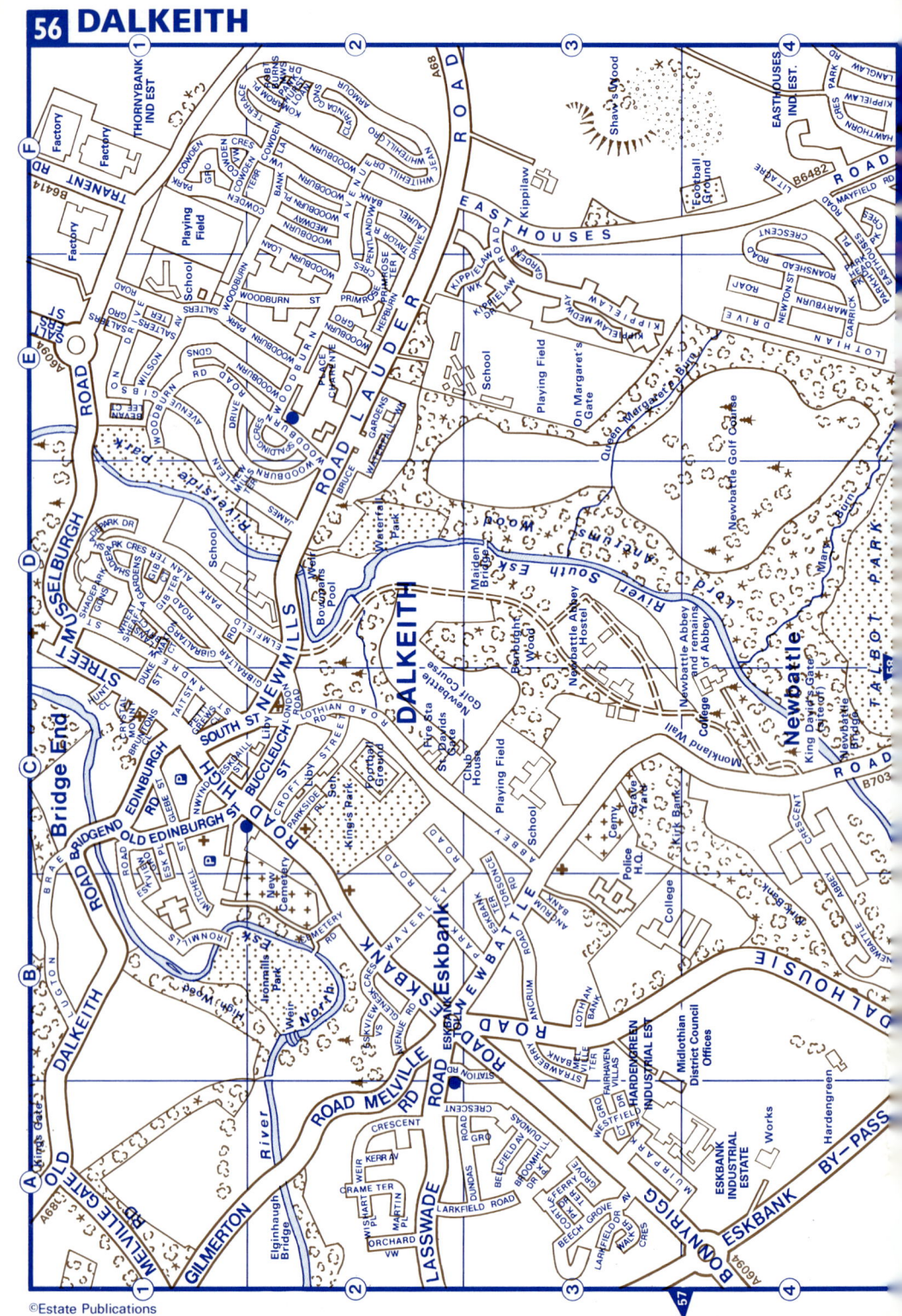

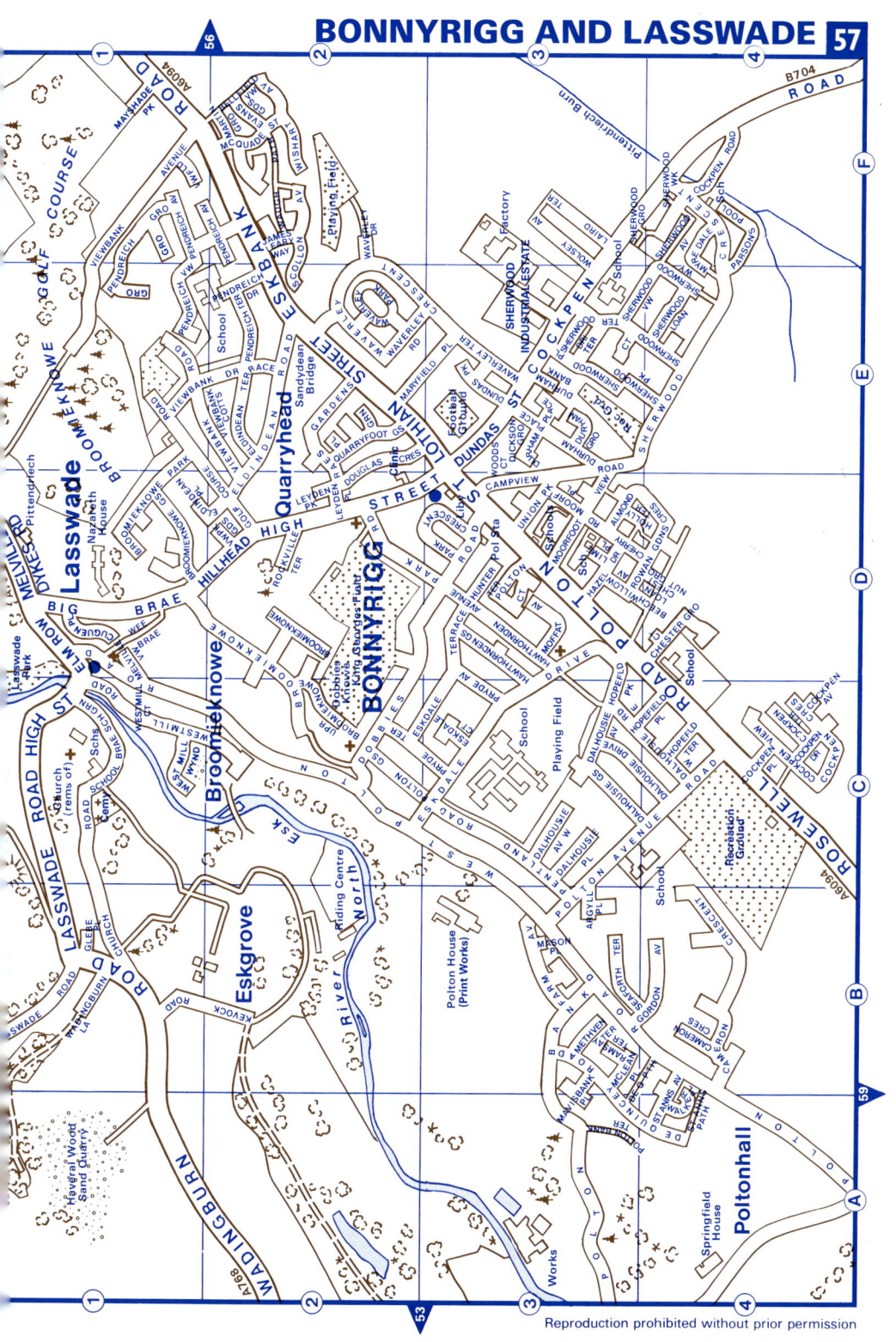

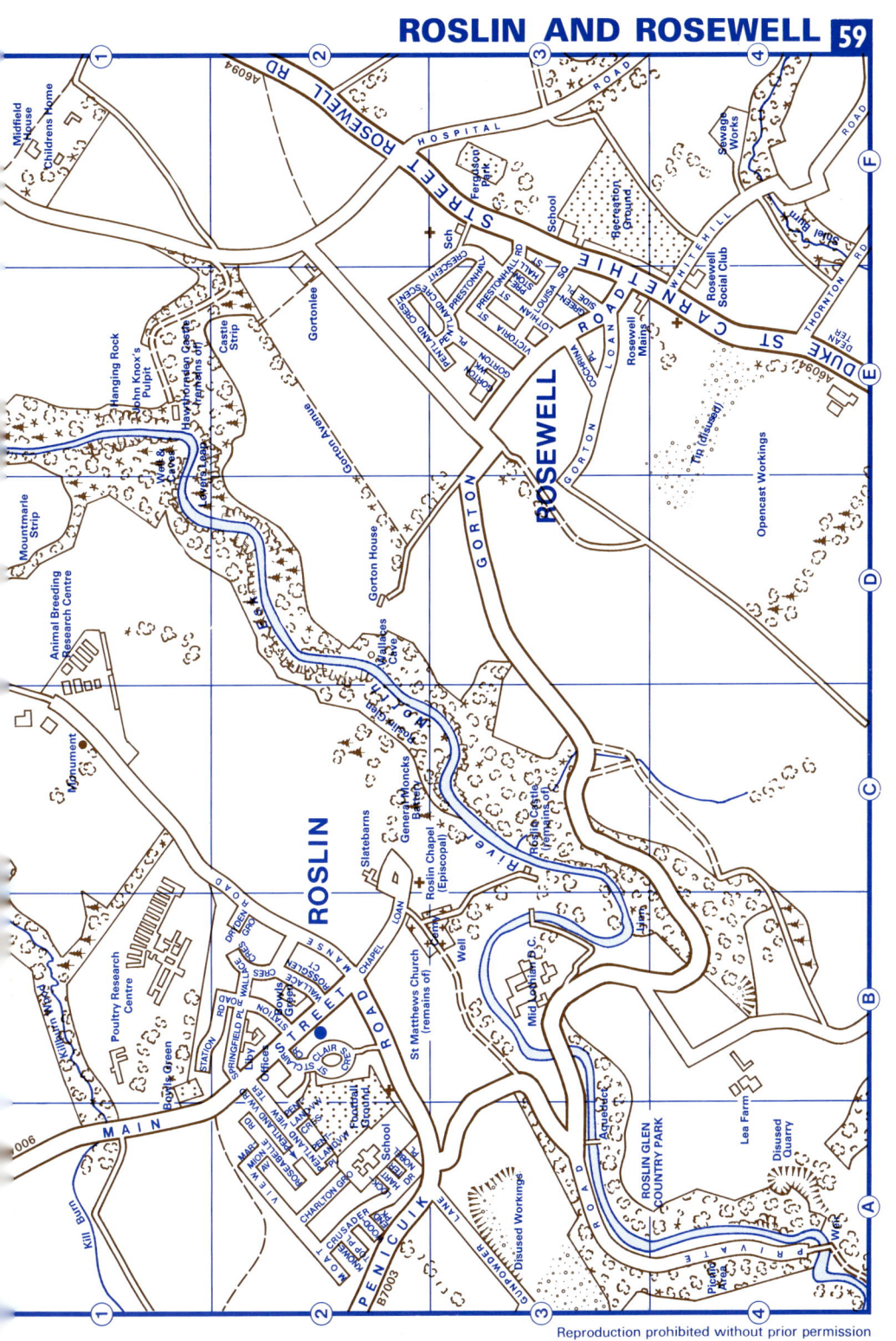

ROSEWELL

ROSLIN

Milton Bridge

Loganbank

Bush
(Centre of Rural Economy)

Glencorse Burn

Glencorse Old Kirk
(remains)

Glencorse House

MILTON BRIDGE
TRAINING CAMP

Parade Ground

Council Depot

School

GRAHAMS

GLENCORSE BARRACKS

BELWOOD CRES

BELWOOD ROAD

CATRIONA TER

BALFOUR TER

HAWKINS TER

LIVESAY TER

GREELY TER

BRECK TER

GREENLAW

ZINKERMAN CT

RAMILLIES CT

CORUNNA CT

SALAMANCA CR

ABRASS GRO

MUIRHEAD ROAD

VICTORIA DRIVE

OYE ORR

BLENHEIM CT

School

MACCORMICK TER

Spring Hill

Crosshouse

A702

Flotterstone Bridge

Flotterstone House

Glencorse Mains

BELWOOD

MAURICEWOOD

Belwood House

Mauricewood

Mauricewood Mains

Mauricewood

VIEW

A701

Bowling Green

Bilston Inn

MYRTLE CR

BILSTON INN PL

MEADOW

STANLEY AV

PARK AV

SEAFIELD ROAD

SCHOOL

School

Rec. Ground

ESKGROVE CRES

MUIR AV

CASTLELAW CRES

CASTLELAW CRES

CARR KELTON AV

MOORFOOT

House o' Muir

Martyrs Cross

Stone Circle
(remains of)

Lawhead Hill

Seafield

BILSTON

Bilston Burn

MOOR ROAD

SEAFIELD
A703

Pentlandfield
(Crop Research Institute)

Turnhouse

Martyrs Monument

Enclosures

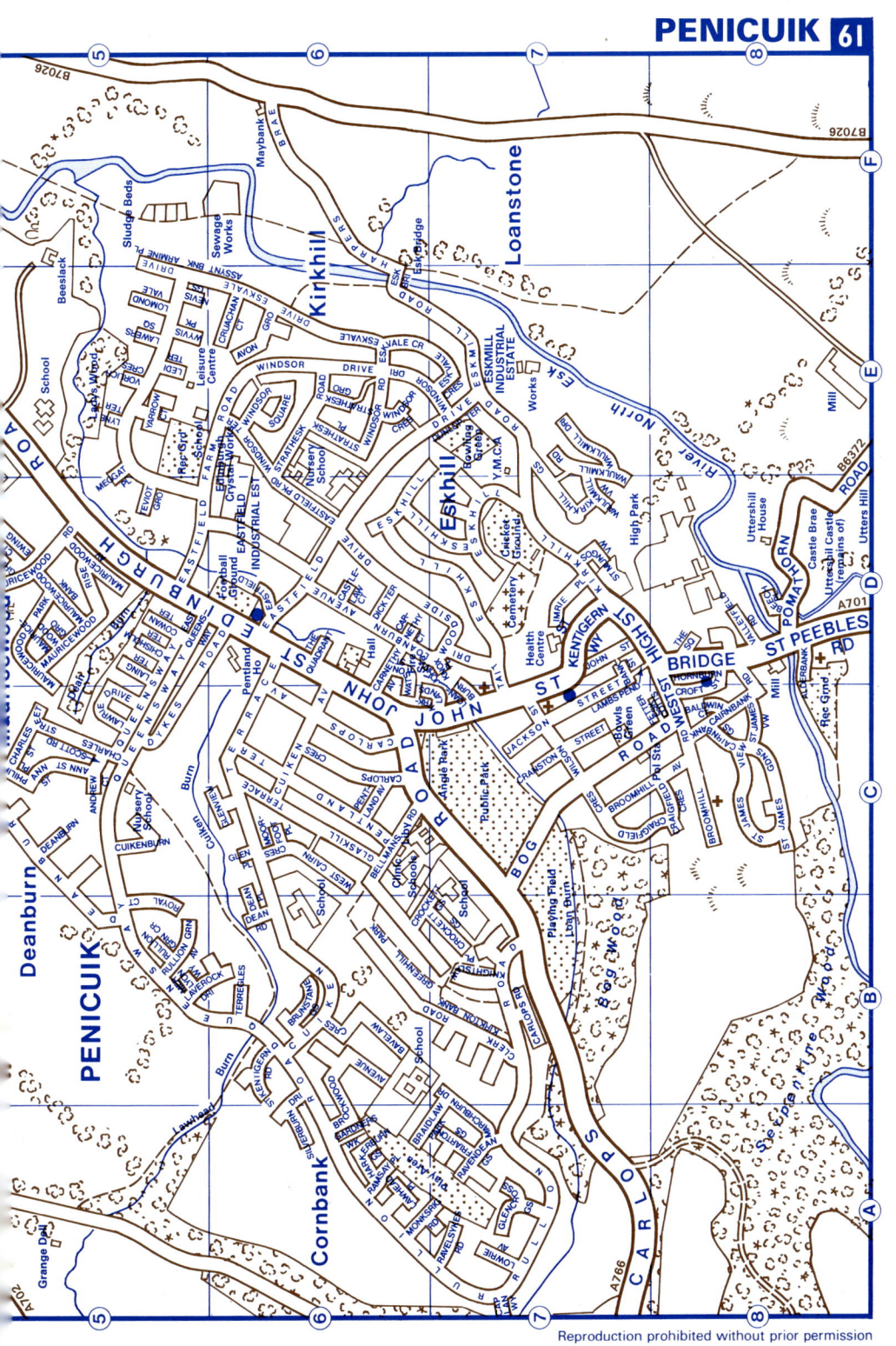

PRESTONPANS

PRESTON

Cuthill

FIRTH OF FORTH

Bells Rock
Cockenzie Harbour
Black Rocks
Jetty
Pier
Cockenzie Power Station
The Humlocks
Whin Park
WHIN PARK IND ESTATE
Whin Park

Slideaway Rocks
Mathew Rocks
Hays Rocks
Hepburn Rocks
Ringans Hple
Dow Craig
Mackie Rocks
Girdle Rocks
Ox Rocks
Cuthill Rocks

Cemetery
Football Ground
Playing Field
Football Ground
High School

Town Hall
Liby
School
Cemy
Football Ground
Bowls
Health Centre
Com Cent
Hawthorn

Miners Welfare
School
School
Meadowmill Sports Cer
Col Gardiners Monument
Works
MID ROAD (PRESTONPANS) INDUSTRIAL ESTATE
PRESTONPANS

Preston Grange Club House
Remains of Bankton
TRANENT BY-PA

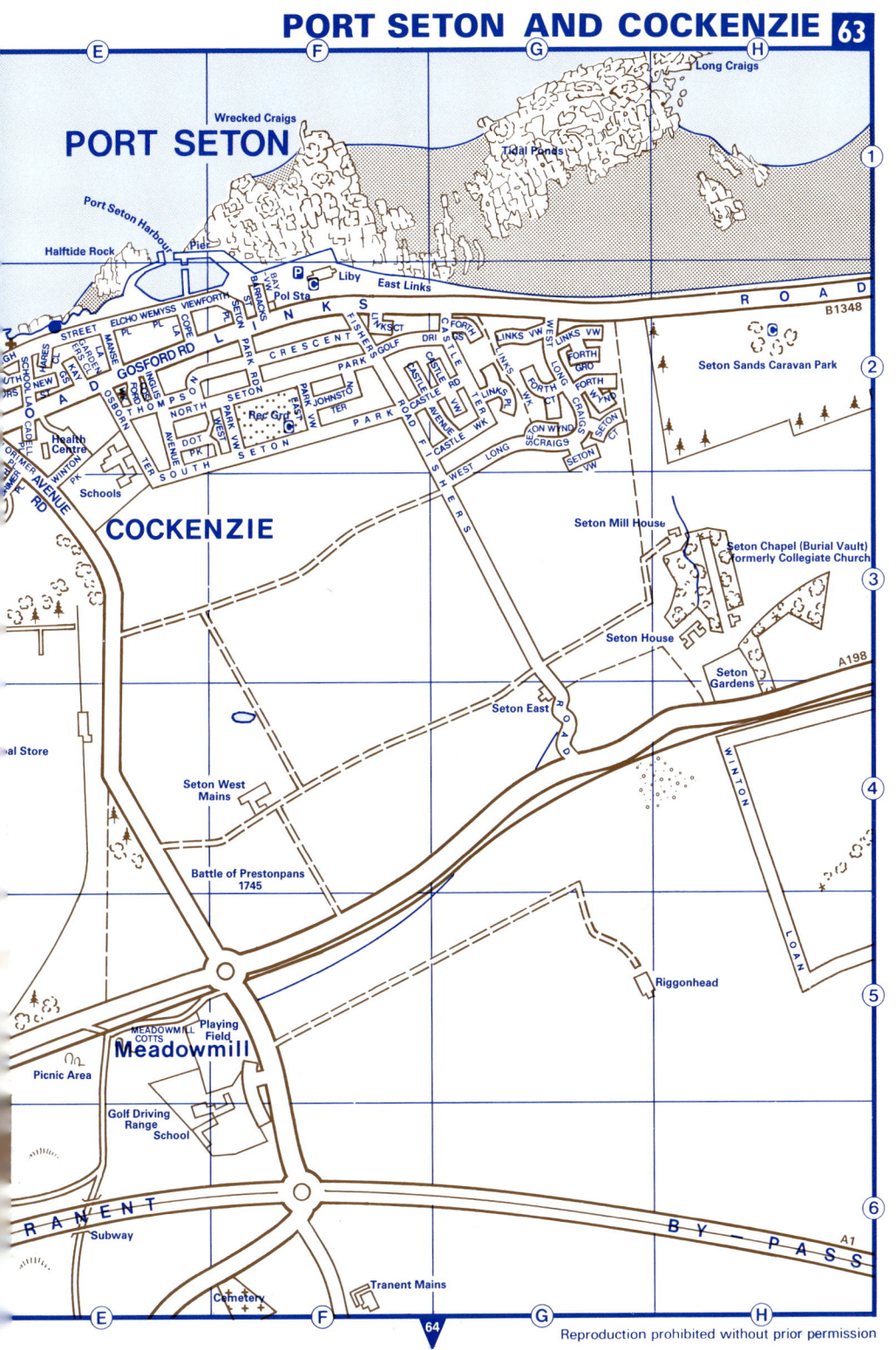

PORT SETON

Long Craigs

Wrecked Craigs

Tidal Ponds

Port Seton Harbour Pier

Halftide Rock

R O A D

B1348

P C Liby East Links
Pol Sta

Seton Sands Caravan Park

BAY VW
ELCHO WEMYSS VIEWFORTH
STREET PL PL COPE
CRES SETON

GOSFORD RD

LINKS VW WEST LINKS VW
FORTH LONG CRAIGS VW
DRI FORTH CRO
LINKSCT FORTH PL
SETON VW
SETON CT
SCRAIGS
LON WYND
SETON VW

Seton Mill House

Seton Chapel (Burial Vault)
formerly Collegiate Church

CRESCENT

FISHERS GOLF
PARK CASTLE
CASTLE AVENUE VW
CASTLE WK
W CASTLE TER

NORTH SETON

PARK JOHNSTO
TER

EAST ST

Rec Grd

PARK WEST

DOT
PK
SOUTH SETON

Schools

COCKENZIE

Health
Centre

WINTON
PK
AVENUE

Seton House

Seton
Gardens

A198

Seton East

F I S H E R S   R O A D

WEST   LONG   ROAD

WINTON

al Store

Seton West
Mains

LOAN

Battle of Prestonpans
1745

Riggonhead

Meadowmill
MEADOWMILL
COTTS
Playing
Field

Picnic Area

Golf Driving
Range
School

T R A N E N T

Subway

B Y - P A S S

A1

Cemetery

Tranent Mains

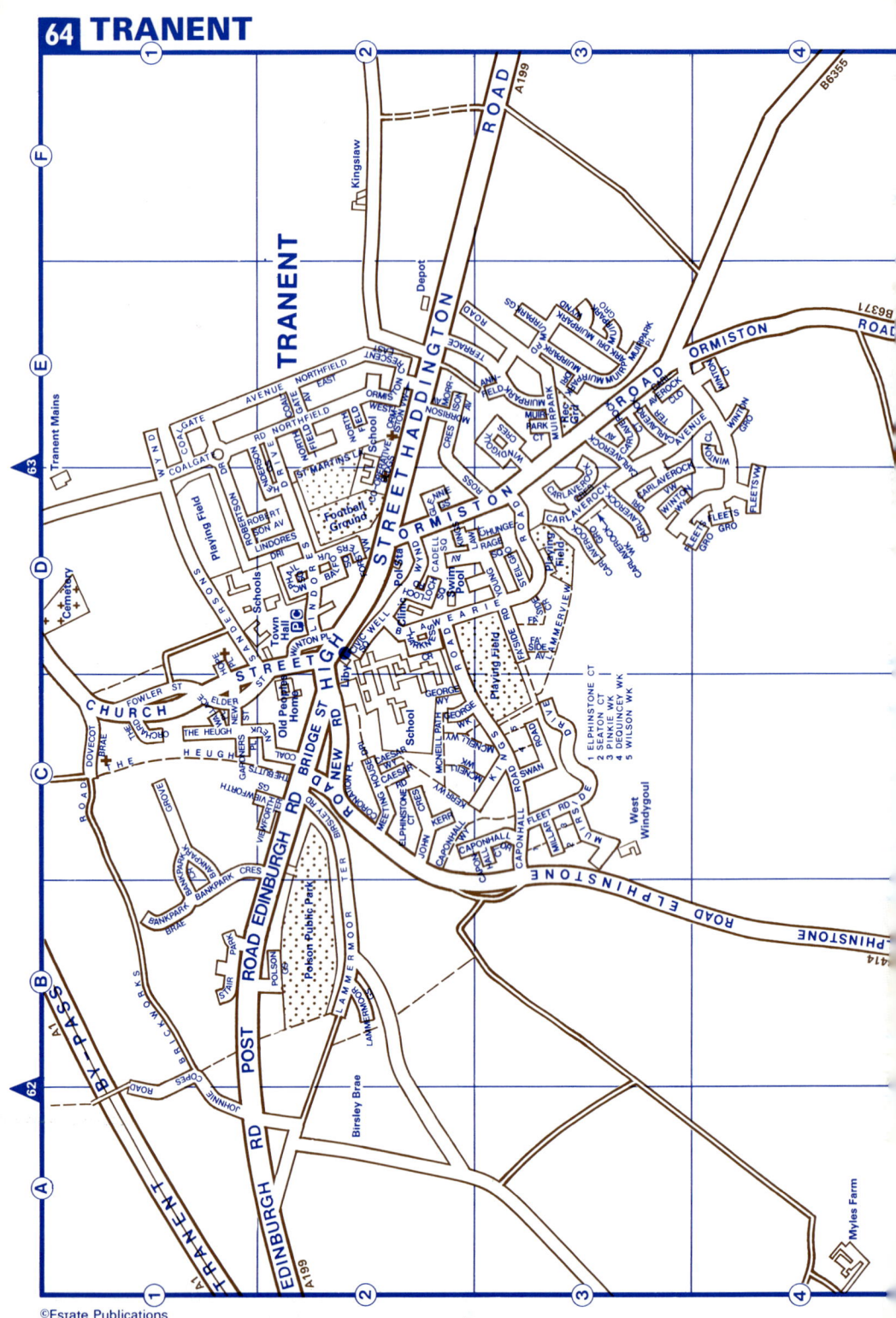

TRANENT

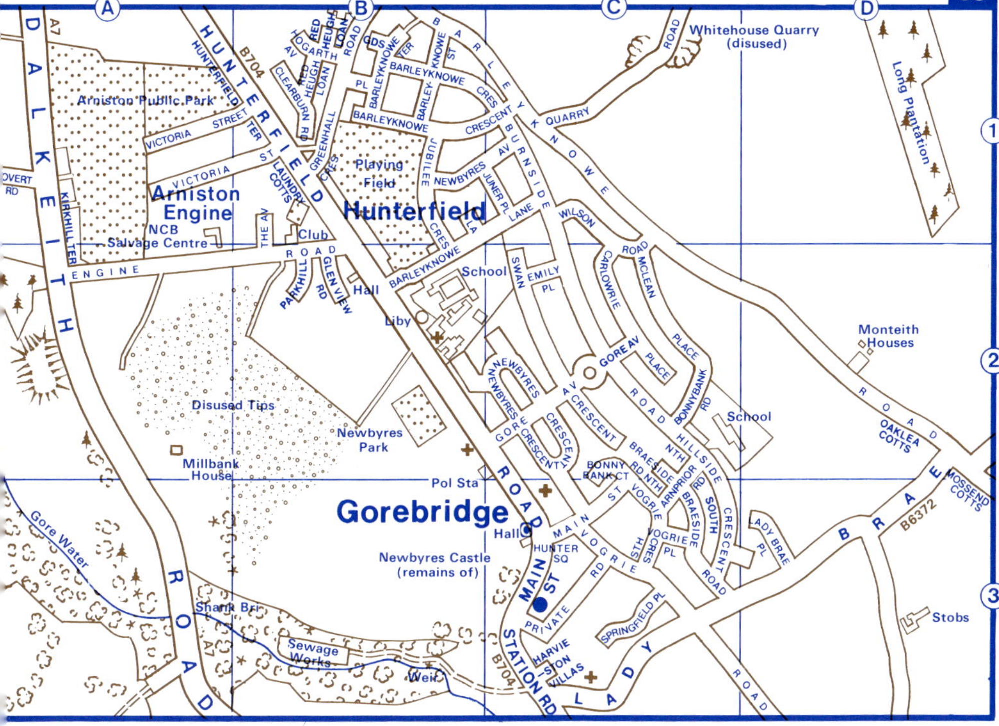

Whitehouse Quarry (disused)

Long Plantation

A7

DALKEITH

B704

HUNTERFIELD

Arniston Public Park

Victoria Street

VICTORIA ST

Arniston Engine

NCB Salvage Centre

ENGINE

OVERT RD

KIRKHILL TER

THE AV

Club

Parkhill Rd

GLENVIEW RD

Hall

Liby

RED HOGARTH LOAN

CLEGHORN LOAN

GREENHALL

HELEN HEUGH

HOGARTH ROAD

GDS

BARLEYKNOWE PL

BARLEYKNOWE CRES

Playing Field

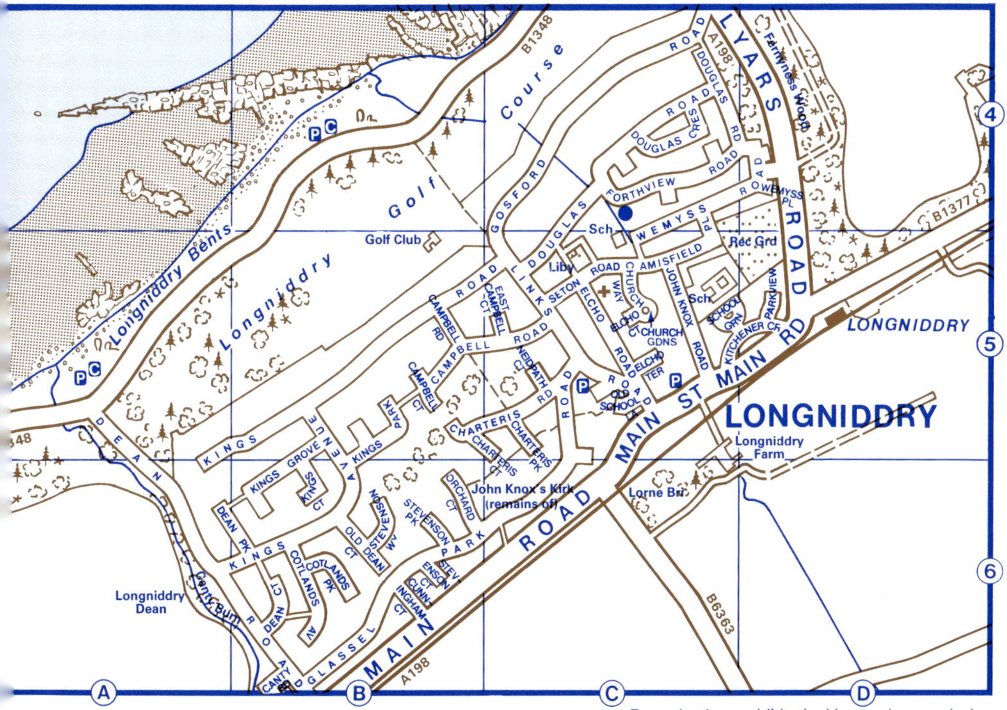

BARLEYKNOWE

Hunterfield

School

BARLEYKNOWE

BARLEYKNOWE ST

JUBILEE

NEWBYRES CRESCENT

JUNIPER LANE

SWAN

BURNSIDE

Quarry

KNOWE

WILSON ROAD

ROAD

GORE AV

EMILY PL

GORE AV

PLACE

PLACE

GORE McLEAN

CARLOWRIE

HILLSIDE

ROAD

BRAESIDE NTH

BONNYBANK RD

School

Monteith Houses

ROAD

OAKLEA COTTS

MOSSEND COTTS

B6372

BRAE

Disused Tips

Millbank House

Newbyres Park

NEWBYRES AV

NEWBYRES CRESCENT

GORE CRESCENT

CRESCENT

GORE CRESCENT

CRESCENT

BRAESIDE

BRAESIDE

SOUTH

ARNPRIOR

BONNY BANK CT

ST VOGRIE

VOGRIE PL

VOGRIE ROAD

CRESCENT

LADY BRAE PL

Gorebridge

Pol Sta

Hall

Newbyres Castle (remains of)

ROAD

MAIN ST

HUNTER SQ

MAIN ST

PRIVATE

HARVIE

SION VILLAS

SPRINGFIELD PL

LADY

ROAD

STATION RD

B704

Gore Water

Shank Br

Sewage Works

Weir

Stobs

B1348

Golf Course

LYARS ROAD

A198

Ferrygate Wood

DOUGLAS RD

DOUGLAS ROADS

DOUGLAS RD

DOUGLAS ROAD

WEMYSS

Wemyss ROW

PC

Golf Club

GOSFORD ROAD

LINKS ROAD

DOUGLAS

NORTHVIEW

Sch

WEMYSS ROAD

Liby

AMISFIELD

Rec Grd

B1377

Longniddry Bents

Longniddry

CAMPBELL RD

EAST CAMPBELL

CAMPBELL

CAMPBELL

SETON

ELCHO

ELCHO

NEWPATH

ELCHO CT

ELCHO ROAD

CHURCH WAY

CHURCH GDNS

ROAD CHESTER

JOHN KNOX ROAD

Sch

School

KITCHENER CR

PARKVIEW

LONGNIDDRY

LONGNIDDRY

MAIN ST

MAIN RD

PC

DEAN

KINGS

KINGS GROVE

KINGS

NASMYTH AVENUE

KINGS

KINGS PARK

DEAN PK

OLD DEAN

COTLANDS PK

COTLANDS

CHARTERIS

CHARTERIS PK

CHARTERIS

ORCHARD

STEVENSON PK

ORCHARD PARK

WY

P

SCHOOL CT

John Knox's Kirk (remains of)

Longniddry Farm

Lorne Br

MAIN ROAD

A198

Longniddry Dean

Gullt Burn

CANTY

GLASSEL

INGHAM

ELCHO CT

B6363

A198

B1348

DEAN PK

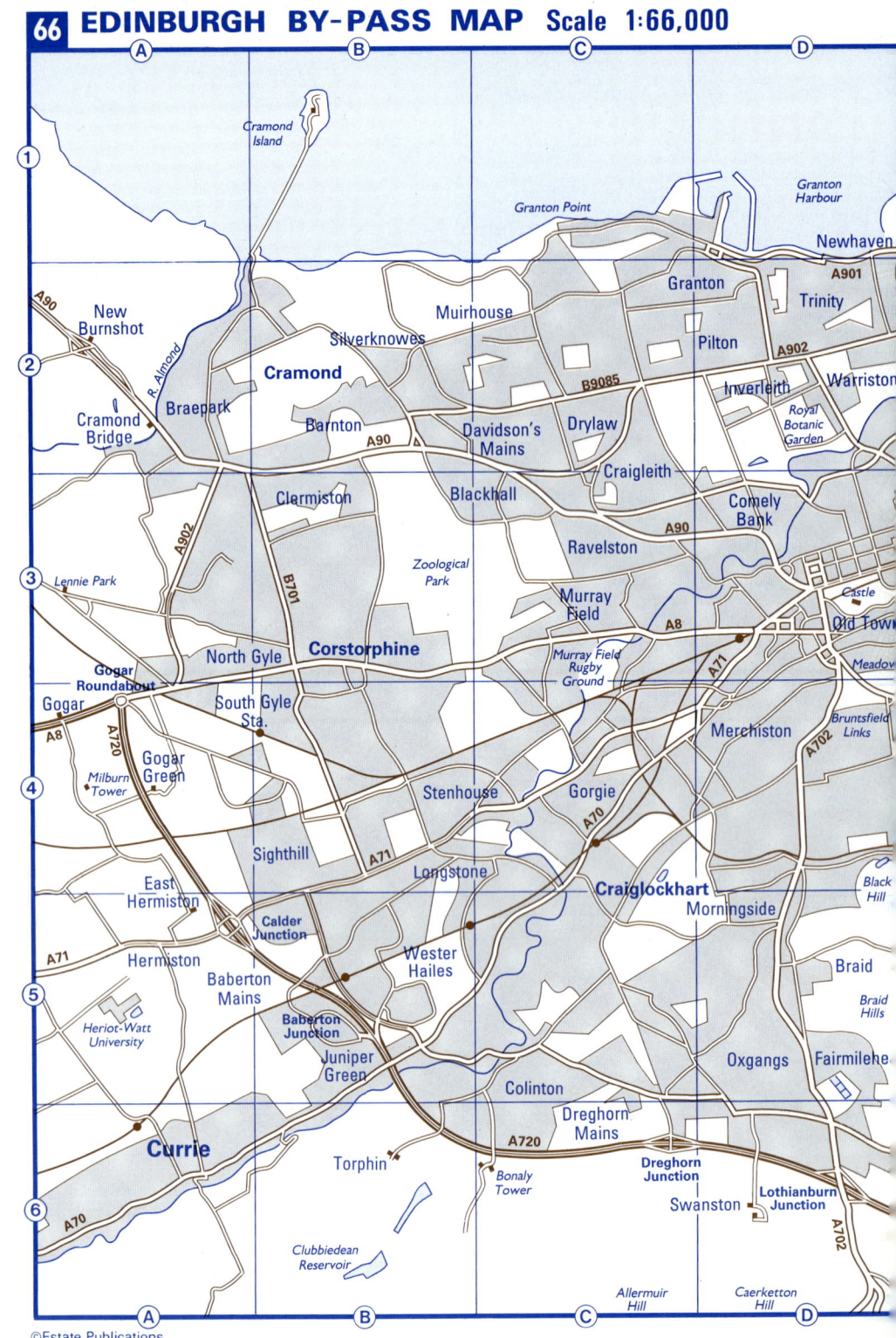

E F G H

1

Leith
Docks

2

orth
eith

Leith

South
Leith

A199

A900

Restalrig

Calton
Hill

A1

Abbeyhill

Portobello

B6415

MUSSELBURGH

3

Waverley
Sta.

Abbey & Palace
of Holyroodhouse

Joppa

Fisherrow

A6124

EDINBURGH

A1

A6106

A1

Newhailes

Holyrood
Park

Duddingston

Arthur's
Seat

Bingham

Newington

Craigmillar

Niddrie

Newcraighall

Monktonhall

4

A7

A68

Bridge
End

Old
Craighall

A1

Nether
Liberton

Royal
Observatory

A7

Little
France

A720

Old Craighall
Junction

A701

Liberton
Dams

Edmonstone

Moredun

A68

Danderhall

A6106

B6415

Millerhill

5

Liberton

Gilmerton

Gilmerton
Junction

A7

A6094

Kaimes

Sherifhall
Roundabout

Sheriffhall

Dalkeith
House

B6414

DALKEITH

6

Burdiehouse

Straiton
Junction

A720

Gilmerton
Junction

Lasswade
Junction

R. North Esk

A68

B6482

umhead
oldings

Straiton

A701

Edgefield

A768

Eskbank

A7

B703

B6482

E F G H

EDINBURGH GLOSSARY

CLOSE -
Gated entrance to Tenement with access to rear of building
COURT - A courtyard
LAND - A Tenement
PEND - An archway
VENNEL - Passage or Lane
WYND - An open thoroughfare

The Index includes some names for which there is insufficient space on the maps. These names are preceded by an * and are followed by the nearest adjoining thoroughfare.

Craighall Av 15 G3
Craighall Bank 15 G3
Craighall Cres 15 F3
Craighall Gdns 15 F3
Craighall Rd 15 F2
Craighall Ter 15 F4
Craighill Gdns 38 C6
Craighouse Av 38 B5
Craighouse Gdns 38 B5
Craighouse Park 38 C6
Craighouse Rd 38 B5
Craighouse Ter 38 B6
Craigievar Sq 21 F5
Craigievar Wynd 21 F5
Craiglea Dri 38 C6
Craiglea Pl 38 B6
Craigleith Av Nth 23 G3
Craigleith Av Sth 23 G4
Craigleith Bank 23 G3
Craigleith Cres 23 G2
Craigleith Dri 23 G3
Craigleith Gdns 23 G3
Craigleith Gro 23 G3
Craigleith Hill 23 H2
Craigleith Hill Av 23 G1
Craigleith Hill Cres 24 A1
Craigleith Hill Gdns 24 A2
Craigleith Hill Grn 23 H1
Craigleith Hill Gro 23 H2
Craigleith Hill Loan 24 A2
Craigleith Hill Park 23 H1
Craigleith Hill Row 23 H2
Craigleith Rise 23 G4
Craigleith Road 24 A2
Craigleith View 23 G4
Craiglockhart Av 37 G5
Craiglockhart Bank 37 G6
Craiglockhart Cres 47 G1
Craiglockhart Dell Rd 37 G6
Craiglockhart Dri Nth 37 G6
Craiglockhart Dri Sth 47 F2
Craiglockhart Gdns 37 G6
Craiglockhart Gro 47 G1
Craiglockhart Loan 37 G6
Craiglockhart Park 47 G1
Craiglockhart Pl 37 H5
Craiglockhart Quadrant 47 G1
Craiglockhart Rd 47 G2
Craiglockhart Rd Nth 37 H6
Craiglockhart Ter 38 B5
Craiglockhart Vw 37 H5
Craigmillar Castle Av 41 F4
Craigmillar Castle Gdns 41 F4
Craigmillar Castle Gro 41 F4
Craigmillar Castle Loan 41 G3
Craigmillar Castle Rd 41 F3
Craigmillar Castle Ter 41 F4
Craigmillar Ct 41 F4
Craigmillar Park 40 B4
Craigmount App 21 H5
Craigmount Av 21 H5
Craigmount Av Nth 21 G2
Craigmount Bank 21 G2
Craigmount Bank Walk 21 G3
Craigmount Bank West 21 G3
Craigmount Brae 21 G3
Craigmount Ct 21 G2
Craigmount Cres 21 G4
Craigmount Dri 21 G4
Craigmount Gdns 21 G5
Craigmount Gro 21 G5
Craigmount Gro Nth 21 G4
Craigmount Hill 21 G3
Craigmount Loan 21 G4
Craigmount Park 21 G5
Craigmount Pl 21 G4
Craigmount Ter 21 G5
Craigmount View 21 G4
Craigmount Way 21 G3
Craigour Av 51 G1
Craigour Cotts 51 H2
Craigour Cres 51 G2
Craigour Dri 51 G1
Craigour Gdns 51 H2
Craigour Grn 51 G2
Craigour Gro 51 G2
Craigour Loan 51 G2
Craigour Pl 51 G1
Craigour Ter 51 G2
Craigpark Av 32 A6
Craigpark Cres 32 A6
Craigs Av 21 G6
Craigs Bank 21 G6
Craigs Cres 21 G6
Craigs Dri 21 G5
Craigs Gdns 21 G5
Craigs Gro 21 H6
Craigs Loan 21 G5
Craigs Park 21 G5
Craigs Rd 20 B4
Cramond Av 11 G3
Cramond Bank 11 G4
Cramond Cres 11 G4
Cramond Gdns 11 G4
Cramond Glebe Gdns 11 G3
Cramond Glebe Rd 11 G2
Cramond Glebe Ter 11 G3
Cramond Grn 11 G3
Cramond Gro 11 G3
Cramond Park 11 G4
Cramond Pl East 11 G3
Cramond Rd Nth 11 G3
Cramond Rd Sth 12 A3
Cramond Regis 11 F5
Cramond Ter 11 G4
Cramond Vale 11 F4
Cramond Village 11 G2
Cranston St 5 F3
Crarae Av 24 A4
Craufordland 11 F6
Crawford Rd 40 B4
Crewe Bank 14 A3
Crewe Cres 14 A3
Crewe Gro 14 A4
Crewe Loan 13 H4
Crewe Pl 14 A3
Crewe Rd Gdns 13 H4
Crewe Rd Nth 13 H3
Crewe Rd Sth 14 A5
Crewe Rd West 13 H3
Crewe Ter 14 A4
Crichton Pl 26 A1
Crichton St 5 E6
Croall Pl 26 A1
Croft-an-Righ 5 H1
Crosswood Av 54 B6
Crosswood Cres 54 B5
Crown Pl 16 B5
Crown St 16 B5
Cuddy La 38 D4
Cultins Rd 35 F4
Cumberland St 25 F2
Cumin Pl 39 H2
Cumlodden Av 23 G4
Cumnor Cres 50 C1
Cunningham Pl 16 B5
Curriehill Castle Dri 54 C2
Curriehill Rd 55 E1
Currievale Dri 54 D2
Currievale Park 54 D2
Currievale Park Gro 54 D2

Daisy Ter 38 B3
Dalgety Av 26 D2
Dalgety Rd 26 D2
Dalgety St 26 D2
Dalhousie Ter 38 D6
Dalkeith Rd 40 B1
Dalkeith St 28 D5
Dalmahoy Cres 54 B3
Dalmahoy Rd, Balerno 54 A1
Dalmahoy Rd, Ratho 32 B6
Dalmeny Rd 15 G4
Dalmeny St 16 B6
Dalry Pl 24 D6
Dalry Rd 24 C6
Dalrymple Cres 39 H3
Dalziel Pl 26 D3
Damside 24 C4
Danderhall Cres 52 C3
Danube St 24 D2
Darnaway St 4 A1
Darnell Rd 14 D4
Davidson Park 14 A6
Davidson Rd 14 A6
Davie St 5 F5
Dean Bank La 25 E2
Dean Bri 24 D3
Dean Park Brae 54 B4
Dean Park Cres 24 D3
Dean Park Mews 24 D2
Dean Park St 24 D2
Dean Path 24 C3
Dean St 24 D2
Dean Ter 24 D2
Deanery Clo 27 E2
Deanhaugh St 25 E2
Deanpark Av 54 B5
Deanpark Ct 54 B5
Deanpark Cres 54 B5
Deanpark Gdns 54 B5
Deanpark Pl 54 B5
Delhaig 37 F3
Dell Rd 47 E3
Denham Green Pl 15 E4
Denham Green Av 15 E4
Derby St 15 G2
Detchmont Rd 21 F6
Devon Pl 24 B6
Dewar Pl 24 D5
Dewar Pl La 24 D5
Dick Pl 39 G3
Dickson St 16 B6
Dicksons Ct 5 E4
Dinmont Dri 40 D6
Distillery La 24 C6
Dochart Dri 21 H3
Dock Pl 16 B3
Dock St 16 B3
Dolphin Av 55 E2
Dolphin Gdns East 55 E2
Dolphin Gdns West 55 E2
Dolphin Rd 55 E2
Dorset Pl 38 C1
Double Hedges Park 50 C1
Double Hedges Rd 50 C1
Douglas Cres 24 C5
Douglas Gdns 24 C4
Douglas Ter 24 C6
Doune Ter 25 E3
Dovecot Gro 47 E1
Dovecot Loan 47 E1
Dovecot Park 47 E2
Dovecot Rd 36 A1
Dowies Mill La 11 E5
Downfield Pl 24 B6
Downie Gro 22 D6
Downie Ter 22 D6
Dreghorn Av 48 B5
Dreghorn Dri 48 A5
Dreghorn Gdns 48 A5
Dreghorn Gro 48 B5
Dreghorn La 48 A5
Dreghorn Loan 47 F4
Dreghorn Park 47 H5
Dreghorn Pl 48 A5
Drum Av 51 H4
Drum Brae Av 21 H4
Drum Brae Ct 21 H3
Drum Brae Cres 21 H2
Drum Brae Dri 21 H3
Drum Brae Gdns 21 H4
Drum Brae Gro 21 H2
Drum Brae Neuk 21 H3
Drum Brae North 21 G1
Drum Brae Park 21 H4
Drum Brae Park App 21 H4
Drum Brae Pl 21 H4
Drum Brae South 21 H4
Drum Brae Ter 21 H3
Drum Brae Walk 21 G3
Drum Cotts 51 H5
Drum Cres 51 H4
Drum Pl 51 H4
Drum St 51 G5
Drum Ter 26 B1
Drum View Av 52 C3
Drumdryan St 4 B6
Drummond Pl 25 G2
Drummond St 5 E4
Drumsheugh Gdns 24 D4
Dryden Gdns 16 A6
Dryden Pl 40 B2
Dryden St 16 A6
Dryden Ter 25 H1
Drylaw Av 23 G1
Drylaw Cres 23 F1
Drylaw Gdns 23 F1
Drylaw Grn 23 F1
Drylaw Gro 23 F1
Drylaw House Gdn 13 F6
Drylaw House Paddock 13 F6
Duart Cres 21 H3
Dublin Meuse 25 G2
Dublin St 4 D1
Dublin St Lane Nth 25 G2
Dublin St Lane Sth 4 D1
Duddingston Av 27 H6
Duddingston Cres 28 B6
Duddingston Gdns Nth 27 H5
Duddingston Gdns Sth 28 A6
Duddingston Gro East 27 H6
Duddingston Gro West 27 H6
Duddingston Loan 27 H6
Duddingston Mains Cotts 28 D6
Duddingston Mills Cotts 27 G5
Duddingston Park 28 B5
Duddingston Park Sth 42 B1
Duddingston Rise 42 A1
Duddingston Road 27 G6
Duddingston Road West 41 F1
Duddingston Row 42 A1
Duddingston Sq East 28 A6
Duddingston Sq West 27 H6
Duddingston View 42 A1
Duddingston Yd 42 B1
Dudgeon Pl 8 E2
Dudley Av 15 H3
Dudley Av Sth 15 H3
Dudley Bank 15 H3
Dudley Cres 15 G3
Dudley Gdns 15 G3
Dudley Gro 15 G3
Dudley Ter 15 G3
Duff St 24 B6
Duff Street La 24 B6
Duke Pl 16 C5
Duke St 16 B5
Dukes Walk 26 D3
Dumbiedykes Rd 5 G4
Dumbryden Dri 36 C6
Dumbryden Gdns 36 C6
Dumbryden Gro 46 C1
Dumbryden Rd 46 C1
Dunard Gdns 39 G4
Dunbar St 4 A6
Dunbars Clo 5 G3
Duncan Pl 16 C5
Duncan St 40 A2
Duncans Gait 36 D6
Dundas Pl 8 E2
Dundas St 25 F1
Dundee Pl 38 D1
Dundee St 38 B1
Dundee Ter 38 B2
Dundonald St 25 F2
Dundrennan Cotts 41 E6
Dunedin St 15 G6
Dunrobin Pl 25 E1
Dunsmuir Ct 36 A1
Dunvegan Ct 11 F5
Durar La 21 H3
Durham Av 27 H6
Durham Dri 28 B6
Durham Gdns Nth 28 A5
Durham Gdns Sth 28 B6
Durham Gro 28 B6
Durham Pl East 28 B5
Durham Pl Lane 28 B5
Durham Pl West 28 A6
Durham Rd Sth 42 B1
Durham Sq 28 A6
Durham Ter 28 A5
Durward Gro 40 D6

Earl Grey St 4 A6
Earl Haig Gdns 15 E3
Earlston Pl 26 C2
East Adam St 5 F5
East Barnton Av 12 B6
East Barnton Gdns 12 C6
East Brighton Cres 28 B4
East Caiystane Pl 48 D5
East Caiystane Rd 48 D5
East Castle Rd 38 C2
East Champanyie 39 H4
East Clapperfield 50 C1
East Claremont St 25 G1
East Croft 32 D5
East Cromwell St 16 B3
East Crosscauseway 5 F6
East Ct, Ravelston 23 G3
East Ct, Craigmillar 41 H4
East Farm of Gilmerton 51 H5
East Fettes Av 14 B5
East Fountainbridge 4 A5
East Hermitage Pl 16 C5
East London St 25 G2
East Market St 5 E3
East Mayfield 40 B3
East Montgomery Pl 26 B2
East Newington Pl 40 A2
East Parkside 40 B1
East Preston St 40 A1
*East Preston St La, East Preston St 40 A1
East Restalrig Ter 16 C5
East Silvermills La 25 E2
East Suffolk Rd 40 B4
East Telferton 28 A3
East Trinity Rd 15 E3
Easter Belmont Rd 23 F5
Easter Currie Ct 55 F2
Easter Currie Cres 55 F1
Easter Currie Pl 55 F1
Easter Currie Ter 55 F1
Easter Drylaw Av 13 G6
Easter Drylaw Bank 13 G5
Easter Drylaw Dri 13 G6
Easter Drylaw Gdns 13 G6
Easter Drylaw Gro 13 G6
Easter Drylaw Loan 13 G6
Easter Drylaw Pl 13 G6
Easter Drylaw View 13 G5
Easter Drylaw Way 13 G6
Easter Haugh 48 B3
Easter Park Dri 12 B5
Easter Park Ho 12 B5
Easter Rd 26 B2
Easter Warriston 15 F4
Eastfield Gdns 29 G5
Eastfield Pl 29 H5
Eastfield Rd 19 E5
Eastfield Ter 29 G5
Eden La 39 E4
Edina Pl 26 B2
Edina St 26 B2
Edinburgh Rd, Cramond Bridge 10 A2
Edinburgh Rd, Newbridge 9 D6
Edmonstone Av 52 C2
Edmonstone Dri 52 C3
Edmonstone Rd 52 B2
Edmonstone Ter 52 C2
Eglinton Cres 24 C5
Eglinton St 24 B6
Egypt Mews 39 F5
Eildon St 15 E6
Eildon Ter 15 E6
Elbe St 16 C4
Elcho Ter 28 D4
Elder St 4 D1
Elder St East 4 D1
Electra Pl 28 B2
Elgin Pl 24 B6
Elgin St Nth 26 B1
Elgin St Sth 26 B2
Elgin Ter 26 B2
Elizafield 15 H5
Ellangowan Ter 41 E6
Ellens Glen Loan 51 E3
Ellens Glen Rd 51 E3
Ellens Rd 51 E4
Ellersly Rd 23 F5
Elliot Gdns 47 G2
Elliot Park 47 G2
Elliot Pl 47 G2
Elliot Rd 47 G2
Elliot St 26 B1
Elm Pl 16 C5
Elm Row 25 H2
Elmwood Ter 16 D6
Eltringham Gdns 37 G3
Eltringham Gro 37 G3
Eltringham Ter 37 G3
Esdaile 39 G3
Esplanade 11 H2
Esplanade Ter 29 E5
Essendean Pl 22 A3
Essendean Ter 22 A3
Essex Brae 11 E5
Essex Park 11 E5
Essex Rd 11 E5
Esslemont Rd 40 B5
Ethel Ter 38 D6
Eton Ter 24 D3
Ettrickdale Pl 25 E1
Ettrick Gro 38 D2
Ettrick Rd 38 C3
Eva Pl 39 H5
Eyre Cres 25 F1
Eyre Pl 25 F1
Eyre Ter 25 F1

Fair-a-Far 11 F4
Fair-a-Far Cotts 11 G3
Fairford Gdns 40 D6
Fairmile Av 49 E5
Fairview Rd 18 D6
Fala Ct 50 D5
Falcon Av 39 E4
Falcon Ct 39 E4
Falcon Gdns 39 E4
Falcon Rd 39 E4
Falcon Rd West 39 E4
Falkland Gdns 22 B3
Farrer Gro 27 H3
Farrer Ter 27 H3
Fauldburn 21 F2
Featherhall Av 22 A6
Featherhall Cres North 22 A6
Featherhall Cres South 22 A6
Featherhall Gro 22 A6
Featherhall Pl 22 A6
Featherhall Rd 22 A6
Featherhall Ter 22 A6
Ferniehill Av 51 G4
Ferniehill Dri 51 H4
Ferniehill Gdns 51 H4
Ferniehill Gro 51 H3
Ferniehill Pl 51 H4
Ferniehill Rd 51 G4
Ferniehill Sq 51 H4
Ferniehill St 51 H4
Ferniehill Ter 51 H4
Ferniehill Way 51 H
Fernielaw Av 46 D
Fernielaw Gdns 46 D
Fernieside Av 51 H
Fernieside Cres 51 G
Fernieside Dri 51 H
Fernieside Gdns 51 G
Fernieside Gro 51 H
Ferry Rd Av 13 G
Ferry Rd Dri 13 H
Ferry Rd Gdns 13 G
Ferry Rd Gro 13 G
Ferry Rd Pl 13 G
Ferry Rd, Bangholm 15 E
Ferry Rd, Drylaw 13 E
Ferryfield 14 C
Festival Sq 4 A
Fettes Av 24 B
Fettes Rise 14 C
Fettes Row 25 F
Fidra Ct 13 E
Figgate Bank 28 C
Figgate La 28 C
Figgate St 28 B
Fillyside Av 27 G
Fillyside Rd 17 G
Fillyside Ter 27 G
Findhorn Pl 40 A

Moorfield Cotts 52 D2
Moray Pl 25 E3
Moredun Dykes Rd 51 G5
Moredun Ho 51 G2
Moredun Park Ct 51 F3
Moredun Park Dri 51 F3
Moredun Park Gdns 51 F3
Moredun Park Grn 51 G3
Moredun Park Gro 51 G4
Moredun Park Loan 51 G3
Moredun Park Rd 51 F3
Moredun Park St 51 G3
Moredun Park View 51 G3
Moredun Park Walk 51 G4
Moredun Park Way 51 G3
Moredunvale Bank 51 F2
Moredunvale Grn 51 F2
Moredunvale Gro 51 F2
Moredunvale Loan 51 F2
Moredunvale Park 51 F3
Moredunvale Pl 51 G2
Moredunvale Rd 51 F3
Moredunvale View 51 F2
Moredunvale Way 51 F2
Morningside Ct 38 D6
Morningside Dri 38 C6
Morningside Gdns 38 B6
Morningside Gro 38 C6
Morningside Park 38 D4
Morningside Pl 38 D4
Morningside Rd 38 D2
Morningside Ter 38 D5
Morrison St 24 D5
Morrisons Clo 5 E3
Morton St 29 E5
Mortonhall Gate 50 A6
Mortonhall Park Av 50 B6
Mortonhall Park Bank 50 C6
Mortonhall Park Cres 50 B6
Mortonhall Park Dri 50 B6
Mortonhall Park Gdns 50 B6
Mortonhall Park Grn 50 B6
Mortonhall Park Gro 50 B6
Mortonhall Park Loan 50 B6
Mortonhall Park Pl 50 C6
Mortonhall Park Ter 50 C6
Mortonhall Park View 50 B6
Mortonhall Park Way 50 B6
Mortonhall Rd 39 G5
Morven St 21 H3
Mossgift Walk 50 C1
Moston Ter 40 B3
Mound Pl 4 C3
Mount Lodge Pl 28 C4
Mount Vernon Rd 50 D2
Mountbarns Gdns 50 D2
Mountcastle 27 G4
Mountcastle Bank 28 A4
Mountcastle Cres 27 G4
Mountcastle Dri Nth 27 G4
Mountcastle Dri Sth 28 A5
Mountcastle Gdns 27 H4
Mountcastle Grn 27 G3
Mountcastle Loan 27 H4
Mountcastle Park 27 H3
Mountcastle Pl 27 G3
Mountcastle Ter 27 G4
Mounthooly Loan 49 F5
Mucklets Rd 43 H4
Muir Wood Cres 45 G5
Muir Wood Dri 45 G6
Muir Wood Gro 45 G6
Muir Wood Pl 45 G5
Muir Wood Rd 45 F6
Muirdale Ter 23 F2
Muirend Av 46 C4
Muirhouse Av 13 F5
Muirhouse Bank 13 E5
Muirhouse Cres 13 F4
Muirhouse Dri 13 E4
Muirhouse Gdns 12 D4
Muirhouse Grn 13 E5
Muirhouse Gro 12 D4
Muirhouse Loan 13 E4
Muirhouse Medway 13 E5
Muirhouse Park 13 E5
Muirhouse Parkway 13 E4
Muirhouse Pl East 13 F5
Muirhouse Pl West 13 F5
Muirhouse Ter 13 E5
Muirhouse View 13 E4
Muirhouse Way 13 F4
Mulberry Pl 15 H4
Munro Dri 46 D6
Munro Pl 25 F1
Murano Pl 26 A1
Murdoch Ter 38 C1
Murieston Cres 38 B1
Murieston Cres La 38 B1
Murieston La 38 B1
Murieston Pl 38 B1
Murieston Rd 38 B1
Murieston Ter 38 B1
Murray Cotts 35 H1
Murray Pl 22 B6
Murrayburn App 46 A1
Murrayburn Dri 46 A1
Murrayburn Gate 46 A1
Murrayburn Gdns 36 B6
Murrayburn Grn 46 B1
Murrayburn Gro 46 B1
Murrayburn Park 46 B1
Murrayburn Pl 46 B1
Murrayburn Rd 46 A1
Murrayfield Av 23 H5
Murrayfield Dri 23 G5
Murrayfield Gdns 23 H5
Murrayfield Pl 23 H5
Murrayfield Rd 23 F4
Musselburgh By-Pass 43 E2
Musselburgh Rd 29 E5
Myreside Ct 38 B5
Myreside Mews 38 B5
Myreside Rd 38 B5
Myrtle Ter 38 B2

Nantwich Dri 17 H6
Napier Rd 38 C2
Nellfield 50 D2
Nelson Pl 25 G2
Nelson St 25 F2
Nether Craigour 51 G1
Nether Craigwell 5 G2
Nether Currie Cres 45 F5
Nether Currie Pl 45 F5
Nether Currie Rd 45 G5
Netherby Rd 14 D3
New Belfield 27 G5
New Broompark 14 B2
New Johns Pl 5 F6
New Kirkgate 16 B4
New La 15 G2
New Liston Rd 8 C4
New Market Rd 37 F5
New Orchardfield 16 A5
*New Orchardfield La, Orchardfield La 16 A5
New Skinners Clo 5 E3
New St, Canongate 5 F2
New St, Holyrood 5 F5
New Tower Pl 28 C3
Newbattle Ter 39 E4
Newbridge Rd 9 D6
Newcraighall 42 C3
Newcraighall Dri 43 F3
Newcraighall Rd 43 E3
*Newhaven Exit, Main St 15 G2
Newhaven Pl 15 G2
Newhaven Rd 15 G2
Newington Rd 40 A2
Newlands Park 40 B3
Newmains Rd 8 D2
Newmills Av 54 C2
Newmills Cres 54 C3
Newmills Gro 54 C2
Newmills Rd 54 C2
Newport St 25 E5
Newtoft St 51 G5
Newton Church Rd 52 C3
Newton St 38 A2
Nicolson Sq 5 E5
Nicolson St 5 E5
Niddrie Cotts 42 D3
Niddrie Farm Gro 41 G3
Niddrie House Av 42 A4
Niddrie House Gdns 42 B4
Niddrie House Gro 42 B4
Niddrie House Park 42 A4
Niddrie House Sq 42 A4
Niddrie Mains Ct 42 A3
Niddrie Mains Dri 41 G3
Niddrie Mains Rd 41 G3
Niddrie Mains Ter 41 G2
Niddrie Marischal Cres 42 A3
Niddrie Marischal Dri 42 A4
Niddrie Marischal Gdns 42 A3
Niddrie Marischal Grn 42 A4
Niddrie Marischal Gro 42 B3
Niddrie Marischal Loan 42 A3
Niddrie Marischal Pl 42 A4
Niddrie Marischal Rd 42 A3
Niddrie Marischal St 42 A3
Niddrie Mill Av 42 B2
Niddrie Mill Cres 42 B2
Niddrie Mill Gro 42 B3
Niddrie Mill Pl 42 B2
Niddrie Mill Ter 42 B3
Niddry St 5 E3
Niddry St Sth 5 E4
Nigel Loan 50 D2
Nile Gro 39 E5
Ninians Row 5 E2
Nisbet Ct 16 D6
Noble Pl 16 D5
North Bank St 4 C3
North Bridge 5 E2
North Bridge Arcade 5 E3
North Bughtlin Bank 21 F3
North Bughtlin Brae 21 F3
North Bughtlin Field 21 F2
North Bughtlin Gate 21 F3
North Bughtlin Park 21 F3
North Bughtlin Pl 21 G3
North Bughtlin Rigg 21 F2
North Bughtlin Road 21 F3
North Bughtlin Side 21 F2
North Cairntow 41 F2
North Charlotte St 4 A2
North East Circus Pl 25 E2
North East Cumberland St La 25 F2
North Fort St 15 H2
North Grays Clo 5 E3
North Greens 42 C2
North Gyle Av 21 F6
North Gyle Dri 21 F6
North Gyle Farm Ct 21 F6
North Gyle Farm La 21 F6
North Gyle Gro 21 E6
North Gyle Loan 21 E6
North Gyle Park 21 F6
North Gyle Rd 21 G5
North Gyle Ter 21 E6
North Hillhousefield 15 H2
North Junction St 16 A3
North Leith Sands 16 A2
North Meadow Walk 4 C6
North Meggetland 38 A4
North Park Ter 24 C1
North Peffer Pl 41 G2
North St 32 B6
North St Andrew St 4 D1
North St Andrew St La 4 D1
North St David St 4 C1
North West Circus Pl 25 E2
North West Cumberland St La 25 F2
Northcote St 24 B6
Northfield Av 27 F4
Northfield Broadway 27 G3
Northfield Circus 27 G4
Northfield Cres 27 G4
Northfield Dri 27 G5
Northfield Farm Av 27 G5
Northfield Farm Rd 27 G4
Northfield Gdns 27 G5
Northfield Gro 27 H5
Northfield Park 27 H4
Northfield Park Gro 27 H4
Northfield Rd 27 F4
Northfield Sq 27 G4
Northfield Ter 27 G4
Northlawn Ct 12 B5
Northlawn Ter 12 B5
Northumberland Pl 25 G2
Northumberland Pl Lane 25 G2
Northumberland St 4 B1
Northumberland St Nth East 25 F2
Northumberland St Nth West La 25 F2
Northumberland St Sth East La 25 F2
Northumberland St Sth West La 4 B1
Northview Ct 13 F4
Norton Park 26 C2
Nottingham Pl 5 E1

Oak La 22 B3
Oakville Ter 16 D6
Observatory Grn 39 H5
Observatory Rd 39 H5
Ochiltree Gdns 51 E1
Ogilvie Ter 38 B3
Old Assembly Clo 5 E3
Old Broughton 25 G2
Old Burdiehouse Rd 53 B2
Old Church La 41 E1
Old Dalkeith Rd, Danderhall 52 A2
Old Dalkeith Rd, Nether Liberton 40 D4
Old Farm Av 47 F4
Old Fishmarket Clo 4 D4
Old Hay Weight 25 F5
Old Kirk Rd 22 B5
Old Liston Rd 9 D6
Old Mill La 40 C6
Old Newmills Rd 54 C2
Old Playhouse Clo 5 F3
*Old Stamp Office Clo, High St 5 E3
Old Tolbooth Wynd 5 F2
Orchard Bank 24 A2
Orchard Brae 24 B2
Orchard Brae Av 24 B3
Orchard Brae Gdns 24 B2
Orchard Brae Gdns West 24 B2
Orchard Brae Way 24 B2
Orchard Cres 24 A3
Orchard Dri 24 A3
Orchard Gro 24 B2
Orchard Pl 24 B2
Orchard Rd 24 A3
Orchard Rd Loan 50 C2
Orchard Rd Sth 24 A3
Orchard Ter 24 A2
Orchard Toll 24 A3
Orchardfield Av 36 B1
Orchardfield La 16 A5
Orchardhead Rd 50 C1
Ormelie Ter 29 E5
Ormidale Ter 23 G5
Ormiston Ter 22 B6
Orrok Park 40 C6
Orrvale 54 C4
Orwell Pl 24 C6
Orwell Ter 24 C6
Osborne Ter 24 B5
Oswald Ct 39 G4
Oswald Rd 39 G4
Oswald Ter 36 A1
Otterburn Park 47 F1
Oxcars Ct 12 D4
Oxcraig St 14 B1
Oxford St 40 A1
Oxford Ter 24 D3
Oxgangs Av 48 B4
Oxgangs Bank 48 B5
Oxgangs Brae 48 C5
Oxgangs Broadway 48 B5
Oxgangs Cres 48 B3
Oxgangs Dri 48 B3
Oxgangs Farm Av 48 A5
Oxgangs Farm Dri 48 A5
Oxgangs Farm Gdns 48 B5
Oxgangs Farm Gro 48 A4
Oxgangs Farm Loan 48 B5
Oxgangs Farm Ter 48 B4
Oxgangs Gdns 48 B4
Oxgangs Grn 48 C4
Oxgangs Gro 48 B3
Oxgangs Hill 48 C4
Oxgangs Ho 48 B4
Oxgangs Loan 48 C3
Oxgangs Medway 48 C5
Oxgangs Park 48 B4
Oxgangs Path 48 B5
Oxgangs Pl 48 B4
Oxgangs Rise 48 B4
Oxgangs Road 48 C5
Oxgangs Road Nth 48 A2
Oxgangs Row 48 B4
Oxgangs St 48 B4
Oxgangs Ter 48 A4
Oxgangs View 48 C5

Paisley Av 27 F4
Paisley Clo 5 E3
Paisley Cres 27 E4
Paisley Dri 27 F5
Paisley Gro 27 F5
Paisley Ter 27 F4
Palmer Pl 55 E1
Palmer Rd 55 E1
Palmerston Pl 24 C4
Palmerston Rd 39 G2
Panmure Clo 5 G3
Panmure Pl 4 B6
Papes Cotts 24 A5
Park Av 28 B5
Park Cres 50 D2
Park Gdns 50 D2
Park Gro 50 D3
Park La 28 B6
Park Pl 15 G2
Park Rd 15 F2
Park Ter 43 F3
Park View 43 F3
Parker Av 27 H3
Parker Rd 27 H3
Parker Ter 27 H3
Parkgrove Av 21 H1
Parkgrove Bank 21 H2
Parkgrove Cres 21 H2
Parkgrove Dri 21 G1
Parkgrove Gdns 21 G2
Parkgrove Grn 21 H2
Parkgrove Loan 21 G1
Parkgrove Neuk 21 H2
Parkgrove Path 22 A2
Parkgrove Pl 22 A1
Parkgrove Rd 21 H1
Parkgrove Row 21 H2
Parkgrove St 22 A1
Parkgrove Ter 21 H2
Parkgrove View 21 H2
Parkhead Av 36 B6
Parkhead Cres 36 C6
Parkhead Dri 36 B6
Parkhead Gdns 36 C5
Parkhead Gro 36 C5
Parkhead Loan 36 C5
Parkhead Pl 36 C5
Parkhead St 36 B5
Parkhead Ter 36 C5
Parkhead View 36 B6
Parkside 9 C6
Parkside St 40 A1
Parkside Ter 40 B1
Parkview Pl 16 D5
*Parliament Sq, Main St 15 G2
Parliament Sq 4 D4
Parliament St 16 B3
Parrotshot 42 C2
Parsons Green Ter 27 E3
Path Brae 8 D3
Paties Rd 47 F2
Pattison St 16 C4
Peacocktail Clo 42 C3
Pearce Av 21 H5
Pearce Gro 21 H5
Pearce Rd 21 H5
Peatville Gdns 46 D1
Peatville Ter 36 D6
Peel Ter 40 B3
Peffer Bank 41 F3
Peffer Pl 41 F3
Peffer St 41 F3
Peffermill Ct 41 F4
Peffermill Rd 40 D4
Peggys Mill Rd 11 F4
Pembroke Pl 24 B6
Pennywell Cotts 13 F3
Pennywell Ct 13 F4
Pennywell Gdns 13 E4
Pennywell Gro 13 E4
Pennywell Medway 13 E3
Pennywell Pl 13 F3
Pennywell Rd 13 F3
Pennywell Villas 13 F3
Pentland Av, Colinton 46 D4
Pentland Av, Currie 55 E2
Pentland Cres 48 D3
Pentland Dri 48 C4
Pentland Gdns 48 C3
Pentland Gro 48 D3
Pentland Pl 55 F2
Pentland Rd 46 D4
Pentland Ter 48 D3
Pentland Ter 48 D3
Pentland View, Currie 55 E2
Pentland View, Fairmilehead 48 C4
Pentland View Ct 55 F2
Pentland View Rd 8 C2
Perth St 25 F1
Peveril Ter 50 C2
Picardy Pl 25 H2
Pier Pl 15 F2
Piersfield Gro 27 F3
Piersfield Pl 27 G3
Piersfield Ter 27 F3
Piershill La 27 F3
Piershill Pl 27 F3
Piershill Sq East 27 F3
Piershill Sq West 27 F3
Piershill Ter 27 F3
Pilrig Cotts 16 A6
Pilrig Gdns 15 H6
Pilrig St 16 A5
Pilton Av 14 A4
Pilton Cres 14 B3
Pilton Dri 14 B3
Pilton Dri Nth 14 B2
Pilton Gdns 14 B3
Pilton Loan 14 B3
Pilton Park 14 B3
Pilton Pl 14 A3
Pipe La 28 B3
Pipe St 28 B3
Pirniefield 17 E5
Pirniefield Bank 17 E5
Pirniefield Gdns 17 E5
Pirniefield Gro 17 E5
Pirniefield Ter 17 E5
Pirrie St 16 B4
Pitlochry Pl 26 C2
Pitsligo Rd 39 E3
Pitt St 15 H4
Pitville St 28 D4
Pitville St La 28 D4
Playfair Steps 4 C3
Pleasance 5 F4
Plewlands Av 38 C6
Plewlands Gdns 38 C5
Plewlands Ter C6
Pleydell Pl 50 D2
Pollocks Clo 4 D4
Polwarth Cres 38 C2
Polwarth Gdns 38 C2
Polwarth Gro 38 C2
Polwarth Park 38 C2
Polwarth Pl 38 C2
Polwarth Ter 38 B4
Ponton St 4 A6
Poplar La 16 C4
Porland Ter 16 A3
Porterfield Rd 24 A1
Portgower Pl 24 D2
Portland St 15 H3

Portobello High St 28 B3
Portobello Rd 27 F3
Portsburgh Sq 4 B5
Potterrow 5 E5
Potterrow Port 5 E5
Prestonfield Av 40 C3
Prestonfield Cres 40 C4
Prestonfield Gdns 40 C3
Prestonfield Rd 40 C3
Prestonfield Ter 40 C3
Priestfield Av 40 D3
Priestfield Cres 40 D3
Priestfield Gdns 40 D3
Priestfield Gro 40 D2
Priestfield Rd 40 C2
Priestfield Rd Nth 40 C2
Primrose Bank Rd 15 E2
Primrose Dri 10 B6
Primrose St 16 C5
Primrose Ter 38 B2
Prince Regent St 16 A3
Princes St 4 A3
Promenade 28 A1
Promenade Ter 28 B2
Prospect Bank 25 F1
Prospect Bank Gdns 16 D6
Prospect Bank Gro 17 E5
Prospect Bank Pl 17 E5
Prospect Bank Rd 16 D5
Prospect Bank Ter 17 E5

Quality St 12 C6
Quality St La 12 C6
Quarry Clo 5 F6
Quarry Cotts 42 C3
Quarry Howe 54 B4
Quayside St 16 B3
Queen Anne Dri 9 E6
Queen Charlotte La 16 C4
Queen Charlotte St 16 C4
Queen St 4 A2
Queen St Gdns East 4 C1
Queen St Gdns West 4 B1
Queens Av 23 F2
Queens Av Sth 23 G2
Queens Bay Cres 29 E6
Queens Cres 40 B3
Queens Dri 5 G5
Queens Gdns 23 G1
Queens Park Av 26 D3
Queens Park Ct 27 E3
Queens Rd 23 G2
Queens Walk 41 H4
Queensferry Rd, Barnton 21 E1
Queensferry Rd, Dean 24 A3
Queensferry Rd, Kirkliston 8 D1
Queensferry St 24 D4
Queensferry St Lane 24 D4
Queensferry Ter 24 B3
Quilts Wynd 16 A4

Radical Rd 5 H5
Raeburn Mews 24 D2
Raeburn Pl 24 D2
Raeburn St 24 D2
Ramsay Gdns 4 C4
Ramsay La 4 C4
Ramsay Pl 28 C3
Randolph Cres 24 D4
Randolph La 25 E4
Randolph Pl 25 E4
Rankeillor St 5 F6
Rankin Av 40 A5
Rankin Dri 40 A5
Rankin Rd 40 A5
Rannoch Gro 22 B3
Rannoch Pl 22 B3
Rannoch Rd 22 A3
Rannoch Ter 22 A3
Ransome Gdns 22 A3
Ratcliff Ter 40 A3
Rathbone Pl 28 C3
Ratho Park Rd 32 C5
Ravelrig Hill 54 A4
Ravelrig Park 54 A4
Ravelrig Rd 54 A1
Ravelston Ct 23 H4
Ravelston Dykes 23 F4
Ravelston Dykes La 23 E4
Ravelston Dykes Rd 23 E3
Ravelston Gdn 23 G4
Ravelston Heights 23 G3
Ravelston Ho Gro 23 G3
Ravelston Ho Loan 23 G3
Ravelston Ho Park 23 G3
Ravelston Ho Rd 23 G3
Ravelston Park 24 B4
Ravelston Pl 24 B3
Ravelston Rise 23 G4
Ravelston Ter 24 B3
Ravenscroft Gdns 51 G5
Ravenscroft Pl 51 G5
Ravenscroft St 51 G5
Ravenswood Av 50 D1
Redbraes Gro 15 H5
Redbraes Pl 15 H5
Redford 47 H4
Redford Av 47 F5
Redford Bank 47 G4
Redford Cres 47 G5
Redford Dri 47 F5
Redford Gdns 47 G4
Redford Gro 47 H4
Redford Loan 47 F5
Redford Neuk 47 H4
Redford Pl 47 H4
Redford Rd 47 F4
Redford Ter 47 G5
Redford Walk 47 G4
Redgauntlet Ter 51 E1
Redhall Av 37 E6
Redhall Bank Rd 47 E1
Redhall Cres 37 E5
Redhall Dri 37 E6
Redhall Gdns 37 E5
Redhall Gro 37 E6
Redhall House Dri 47 F1
Redhall Pl 37 E6
Redhall View 37 F6
Redheughs Av 35 F3
Redheughs Muir 35 F3
Redheughs Rigg 35 F2
Reford Pl 47 H4
Regent Pl 26 C2
Regent Rd 5 F2
Regent St 28 C4
Regent St La 28 C3
Regent Ter 5 G2
Regent Ter Mews 5 H1
Regents Gate 40 B1
Regis Ct 11 F5
Register Pl 4 D2
Reid Ter 24 D1
Reids Clo 5 G3
Reids Ct 5 G3
Relugas Gdns 40 A4
Relugas Pl 39 H4
Relugas Rd 39 H4
Research Av One 45 E2
Research Av Two 45 E2
Research Park Rd 45 E3
Restalrig Av 27 E2
Restalrig Circus 17 E6
Restalrig Cres 17 E6
Restalrig Dri 27 E2
Restalrig Gdns 27 E1
Restalrig Ho 27 E1
Restalrig Park 16 D6
Restalrig Rd 16 D5
Restalrig Rd Sth 27 E2
Restalrig Sq 27 E1
Restalrig Ter 16 C5
Riccarton Av 55 F1
Riccarton Cres 55 F1
Riccarton Dri 55 F1
Riccarton Gro 55 F1
Riccarton Mains Rd 45 E1
Richmond Gdns 51 E1
Richmond La 5 F5
Richmond Pl 5 F5
Richmond Ter 24 C6
Riddles Ct 4 D4
Riding Park 11 F5
Riego St 4 A6
Rillbank Cres 39 G1
Rillbank Ter 39 G1
Ringwood Pl 50 D1
Rintoul Pl 25 E1
Riselaw Cres 48 D3
Riselaw Pl 48 D2
Riselaw Rd 48 D2
Riselaw Ter 48 D2
Ritchie Pl 38 B2
Riversdale Cres 23 G6
Riversdale Gro 23 G6
Riversdale Rd 23 F6
Riverside 9 C6
Riverside Rd 10 C5
Robbs Loan 37 G3
Robbs Loan Gro 37 G3
Robert Burns Dri 50 C1
Robertson Av 38 A2
Robertsons Clo 5 E4
Robertsons Ct 5 H2
Rocheid Pk 14 B5
Rochester Ter 38 D3
Roddinglaw Rd 33 G3
Rodney St 25 G1
Ronaldsons Wharf 16 B3
Rose Ct 12 B5
Rose Park 15 E4
Rose St 4 A3
Rose St North La 4 A3
Rose St South La 4 A3
Rosebank Cotts 24 D6
Rosebank Gdns 14 D4
Rosebank Gro 14 D4
Rosebank Rd 14 D4
Rosebery Cres 24 C5
Rosebery Cres La 24 C5
Roseburn Av 23 H6
Roseburn Cliff 24 A5
Roseburn Cres 23 H6
Roseburn Dri 24 A6
Roseburn Gdns 24 A5
Roseburn Pl 24 A5
Roseburn St 24 A6
Roseburn Ter 24 A5
Rosefield Av 28 B4
Rosefield Av La 28 B4
Rosefield La 28 B4
Rosefield Pl 28 B4
Rosefield St 28 B4
Rosemount Bldgs 24 D6
Roseneath Ter 39 G1
Rosevale Pl 16 D5
Rosevale Ter 16 C5
Roseville Gdns 15 F3
Ross Gdns 40 A5
Ross Pl 40 A5
Ross Rd 40 B6
Rossie Pl 26 B2
Rosslyn Cres 16 A6
Rosslyn Ter 16 A6
Rothesay Mews 24 C4
Rothesay Pl 24 C4
Rothesay Ter 24 C4
Roull Gro 36 B2
Roull Pl 36 B2
Roull Rd 36 B2
Rowan Tree Av 54 D2
Rowan Tree Gro 54 D2
Rowan Tree Pl 54 D3
Roxburgh Pl 5 F4
Roxburgh St 5 F4
Royal Circus 25 E2
Royal Cres 25 F2
Royal Mile 5 E3
Royal Park Pl 26 D3
Royal Park Ter 26 D3
Royal Ter 26 A2
Royston Mains Av 14 A3
Royston Mains Cres 13 H3
Royston Mains Gdns 14 A3
Royston Mains Grn 14 A3
Royston Mains Pl 14 A3
Royston Mains Rd 14 A2
Royston Mains St 14 A3
Royston Ter 15 E5
Russell Pl 15 E3
Russell Rd 24 A6
Rustic Cotts 47 F4
Rutherford Dri 50 D1
Rutland Ct 25 E5
Rutland Sq 25 E5
Rutland St 25 E4
Ryehill Av 16 D6
Ryehill Gdns 16 D6
Ryehill Gro 16 D6
Ryehill Pl 16 D5
Ryehill Ter 16 D5

Saddletree Loan 41 E6
St Albans Rd 39 G4
St Andrew Pl 16 C5
St Andrew Sq 4 D1
St Anthonys Pl 16 B4
St Anthonys St 16 B4
St Berenards Cres 24 D2
St Bernards Bri 24 D2
St Bernards Row 25 E2
St Catherines Gdns 22 D6
St Catherines Pl 39 H2
St Clair Av 16 B6
St Clair Pl 16 B6
St Clair Rd 16 C6
St Clair St 16 B6
St Clair Ter 38 C6
St Colme St 25 E3
St Davids Pl 24 D5
St Davids Ter 24 D5
St Fillans Ter 38 C6
St James Pl 4 D1
St James Sq 4 D1
St John St 5 F3
St Johns Av 22 C6
St Johns Cres 22 C6
St Johns Gdns 22 C6
St Johns Hill 5 F4
St Johns Pl 16 C4
St Johns Rd 22 A6
St Johns Ter 22 C6
St Katharines Brae 50 C4
St Katharines Cres 50 C5
St Katharines Loan 50 D5
St Leonards Bank 5 G6
St Leonards Cragg 5 G6
St Leonards Hill 5 G6
St Leonards La 5 G6
St Leonards St 5 F6
St Margarets Rd 39 E3
St Marks La 28 C4
St Marks Pl 28 C4
St Marys Pl 28 D5
St Marys Pl Lane 28 D4
St Marys St 5 F3
St Ninians Dri 22 A6
St Ninians Rd 22 A6
St Ninians Ter 38 C6
St Patrick Sq 5 F6
St Patrick St 5 F6
St Peters Bldgs 38 D1
St Peters Pl 38 D1
St Ronans Ter 38 C6
St Stephens Pl 25 E2
St Stephens St 25 E2
St Teresa Pl 38 C3
St Thomas Rd 39 H4
St Vincent St 25 F2
Salamander Pl 16 D4
Salamander St 16 C3
Salisbury Pl 40 A2
Salisbury Rd 40 A2
Salmond Pl 26 C2
Salvesen Ter 13 F3
Salveson Cres 13 E3
Salveson Gdns 13 E3
Salveson Gro 13 E3
Sand Port 16 B3
Sandford Gdns 28 B4
Sandport Pl 16 B3
Sandport St 16 B3
Sauchiebank 24 B6
Saughton Av 37 G2
Saughton Cres 23 E6
Saughton Gdns 23 F6
Saughton Gro 23 F6
Saughton Hall Gdns 23 G6
Saughton Loan 23 F6
Saughton Mains Av 36 D3
Saughton Mains Bank 36 D3
Saughton Mains Dri 36 C4
Saughton Mains Gdns 36 C4
Saughton Mains Gro 36 D4
Saughton Mains Loan 36 C4
Saughton Mains Park 36 C3
Saughton Mains Pl 36 C4
Saughton Mains St 36 C3
Saughton Mains Ter 36 D3
Saughton Park 23 F6
Saughton Rd 36 C3
Saughton Rd Nth 36 B1
Saughtonhall Av 37 F1
Saughtonhall Av West 37 F1
Saughtonhall Circus 23 F6
Saughtonhall Cres 23 F6
Saughtonhall Dri 23 F6
Saughtonhall Gro 23 F6
Saughtonhall Pl 23 F6
Saughtonhall Ter 23 F6
Saunders St 25 E2
Savile Pl 40 A4
Savile Rd 40 B4
Savile Ter 40 B4
Saxe Coburg Pl 25 E1
Saxe Coburg St 25 E1
*Saxe Coburg Ter, Saxe Coburg St 25 E1
School Brae Row 11 G3
School House Pl 40 A2
School Wynd 32 B5
Sciennes 39 H1
Sciennes Gdns 39 H2
*Sciennes Hill Pl, Sciennes Gdns 39 H2
Sciennes Hill Rd 39 H2
Sciennes Rd 39 G2
Scone Gdns 27 E3
Scotland St 25 G1
Scotsman Bldgs 5 E3
Seacot 17 F5
Seafield Av 17 E5
Seafield Pl 17 E5
Seafield Rd 17 E4
Seafield Rd East 17 G5
Seafield St 17 F5
Seafield Ter 17 E5
Seafield Way 17 H6
Seaforth Dri 23 F2
Sealcarr St 14 A1
Seaport St 16 C3
Seaview Cres 29 F5
Seaview Ter 29 F5
Second Gait 44 D2
Semple St 4 A5
Seton Pl 39 H2
Shaftesbury Park 38 A3
Shandon Cres 38 A3
Shandon Pl 38 A3
Shandon Rd 38 A3
Shandon St 38 A3
Shandon Ter 38 A3
Shanter Way 50 C1
Shanwick Pl 25 E4
Sharpdale Loan 40 C5
Shawfair Rd 52 D1
Shaws Pl 16 A6
Shaws Ter 16 A6
Sheriff Brae 16 B3
Shore 16 B3
Shore Pl 16 B3
Shrub Mount 28 B3
Shrub Pl 26 A1
Shrub Place La 26 A1
Sienna Gdns 39 H2
Sighthill Av 36 B6
Sighthill Bank 36 A5
Sighthill Ct 36 A5
Sighthill Cres 36 A6
Sighthill Dri 46 A1
Sighthill Gdns 36 B6
Sighthill Grn 36 A5
Sighthill Gro 36 B6
Sighthill Loan 36 A6
Sighthill Neuk 36 A6
Sighthill Park 36 B6
Sighthill Pl 36 A6
Sighthill Rise 46 A1
Sighthill Rd 36 A6
Sighthill St 36 A6
Sighthill Ter 36 A6
Sighthill View 36 A6
Sighthill Wynd 36 B5
Silverknowes Av 12 C5
Silverknowes Bank 12 D5
Silverknowes Brae 12 D5
Silverknowes Ct 12 D4
Silverknowes Cres 12 C5
Silverknowes Dell 12 D6
Silverknowes Dri 12 C5
Silverknowes Eastway 12 D4
Silverknowes Gdns 12 D4
Silverknowes Grn 12 D5
Silverknowes Gro 12 D4
Silverknowes Hill 12 C5
Silverknowes Loan 12 C5
Silverknowes Midway 12 D5
Silverknowes Neuk 13 E6
Silverknowes Parkway 12 D4
Silverknowes Pl 12 D4
Silverknowes Rd 12 C2
Silverknowes Rd East 12 D5
Silverknowes Rd Sth 12 D6
Silverknowes Southway 13 E5
Silverknowes Ter 12 C5
Silverknowes View 12 D5
Simon Sq 5 F6
Sir Harry Lauder Rd 28 A3
Sir William Fraser Homes 47 E3
Slateford Rd 37 G5
Slaeside 54 B4
Sleigh Dri 26 D1
Sleigh Gdns 27 E1
Sloan St 16 B6
Smithfield St 38 A2
Smiths Pl 16 B5
Smithy Green Av 52 C3
Somerset Pl 16 C5
South Barnton Av 12 B6
South Beechwood 23 E6
South Bridge 5 E3
South Charlotte St 4 A3
South Clerk St 40 A1
South College St 5 E5
South East Circus Pl 25 E2
South East Cumberland St La 25 F2
South Ettrick Rd 38 C3
South Fort St 15 H4
South Gillsland Rd 38 C4
South Gray St 40 A3
South Grays Clo 5 E3
South Groathill Av 23 G2
South Gyle Access 35 H3
South Gyle Broadway 34 D1
South Gyle Cres 35 F2
South Gyle Gdns 35 G1
South Gyle Loan 35 G2
South Gyle Mains 35 G2
South Gyle Park 35 G
South Gyle Rd 35 F
South Gyle Wynd 35 H
South Lauder Rd 39 H
South Learmonth Av 24 C
South Learmonth Gdns 24 C
South Lorne Pl 16 B
South Maybury 21 E
South Mellis Park 27 G
South Morton St 29 E
South Oswald Rd 39 F
South Oxford St 40 A
South Park 15 G
South Sloan St 26 B
South St Andrew St 4 D
South St Davids St 4 D
South Trinity Rd 15 E
South West Cumberland St La 25 F
Southbank 12 B
Southbank Ct 12 B
Southfield Bank 28 A
Southfield Farm Gro 27 H

Mayburn Hill 53 B5
Mayburn Loan 53 B4
Mayburn Ter 53 B4
Mayburn Vale 53 B5
Mayburn Walk 53 B5
Mayfield Ct 53 D5
Mayfield Cres 53 C5
Mayshade Rd 53 B4
Muirfield Gdns 53 C5
New Pentland Ind Est 53 A6
Nivens Knowe Rd 53 A6
Paradykes Av 53 B5
Park Av 53 B6
Park Cres 53 B6
Park View 53 B6
Pentland Rd 53 A5
Polton Rd 53 C6
Station Rd 53 C5
Straiton Rd 53 A5
The Loan 53 B6
Traprain Ter 53 D6

LONGNIDDRY

Amisfield Pl 65 C5
Campbell Ct 65 B5
Campbell Rd 65 B5
Canty Rd 65 B6
Charteris Ct 65 B5
Charteris Pk 65 C5
Charteris Rd 65 B5
Church Gdns 65 C5
Church Way 65 C5
Cotlands Av 65 B6
Cotlands Pk 65 B6
Cunningham Ct 65 B6
Dean Ct 65 B6
Dean Park 65 B6
Dean Rd 65 A5
Douglas Cres 65 C4
Douglas Rd 65 C4
East Campbell Ct 65 C5
Elcho Ct 65 C5
Elcho Rd 65 C5
Elcho Ter 65 C5
Forthview Rd 65 C4
Glassel Park Rd 65 B6
Gosford Rd 65 C4
John Knox Rd 65 C5
Kings Av 65 B6
Kings Ct 65 B5
Kings Gro 65 B5
Kings Park 65 B5
Kings Rd 65 B5
Kitchener Cres 65 C5
Links Rd 65 C5
Lyars Rd 65 C4
Main Rd 65 B6
Main St 65 C5
Neidpath Ct 65 C5
Old Dean Ct 65 B6
Old School La 65 C5
Orchard Ct 65 B6
Parkview 65 D5
School Grn 65 C5
Seton Rd 65 C5
Stevenson Ct 65 B6
Stevenson Pk 65 B6
Stevenson Way 65 B6
Wemyss Pl 65 D4
Wemyss Rd 65 C4

MUSSELBURGH/ WALLYFORD

Albert Cres 31 H3
Albert Pl 31 H3
Ashgrove Pl 31 E2
Ashgrove 31 E2
Ashgrove Vw 31 E2
Balcarres Pl 30 D1
Balcarres Rd 30 D1
Beach La 30 B1
Beaulah 31 E2
Beggers Bush 31 G1
Bellfield Av 30 B2
Bellfield Ct 30 B3
Bog Park Rd 30 A2
Bridge St 30 C2
Bush St 30 B1
Bush Ter 30 B2
Cairds Vw 30 B1
Campie Gdns 30 B2
Campie Rd 30 B2
Carberry Rd 30 D4
Carly Pl 30 C2
Champigny Ct 31 E3
Church La 30 C3
Clayknowes Dri 30 A3
Clayknowes Pl 30 A3
Clayknowes Way 30 A3
Cottage La 31 E3
Cowpits Rd 30 D6
Craighill Ter 31 F2
Crookston Rd 31 E4
Dalrymple Cres 30 A2
Dalrymple Loan 30 C2
Delta Av 31 F3
Delta Cres 31 G2
Delta Dri 31 G2
Delta Gdns 31 G3
Delta Pl 30 D4
Delta Rd 31 G3
Delta Vw 31 G2
Double Dykes 30 D4
Downie Pl 30 C2
Drummohr Av 31 G3
Drummohr Gdns 31 G3
Edenhall Bank 31 E3
Edenhall Cres 31 E3
Edenhall Rd 31 E3
Edinburgh Rd 30 A1
Eskmill Villas 30 B3
Eskside East 30 C2
Eskside West 30 B3
Eskview Av 30 B3
Eskview Cres 30 B3
Eskview Gro 30 B3
Eskview Rd 30 B3
Eskview Ter 30 B3
Fa'side Av Nth 31 G4
Fa'side Av Sth 31 G4
Fa'side Ct 31 H4
Fa'side Cres 31 G4
Fa'side Dri 31 G4
Fa'side Gdns 31 H4
Fa'side Ter 31 H4
Fishers Wynd 30 B2
Forthview Av 31 G3
Forthview Cres 31 G3
Forthview Dri 31 G3
Forthview Ter 31 G3
Galt Cres 31 F3
Galt Dri 31 G2
Galt Rd 31 G3
Galt Ter 31 G3
Goose Grn 30 D1
Goose Grn Av 30 D1
Goose Grn Cres 30 D1
Goose Grn Pl 30 D1
Goose Grn Rd 30 D1
Gracefield Ct 30 C2
Grove St 30 D3
Haddington Rd 31 G2
Harbour Rd 30 B2
Hercus Loan 30 B2
High St 30 C2
Hope Pl 31 F2
Inchview Cres 31 H3
Inchview Rd 31 H3
Inveravon Ter 30 C3
Inveresk Rd 30 C3
Inveresk Village Rd 30 D3
James St 30 D2
Kerrswynd 30 D2
Kilwinning Pl 30 D2
Kilwinning St 30 D2
Kilwinning Ter 30 D2
King St 30 D3
Ladywell 30 C2
Ladywell Way 30 C2
Lewisvale Av 31 E3
Lewisvale Ct 31 E3
Linkfield Rd 30 D2
Links Av 30 B1
Links St 30 C2
Links View 30 C1
Lochend Rd Nth 30 B2
Lochend Rd Sth 30 B2
Lorretto Ct 30 B4
Macbeth Moir Rd 31 F2
Maitland Av 30 A2
Maitland Park 30 A2
Maitland Rd 30 A2
Maitland St 30 A2
Mall Av 30 C2
Mansfield Av 30 D3
Mansfield Ct 30 D3
Mansfield Pl 30 C3
Mansfield Rd 30 C2
Market St 30 B2
Mayfield Av 30 B5
Mayfield Cres 30 B4
Mayfield Park 30 B5
Mayfield Pl 30 B5
Mayville Bank 31 G2
Millhill 30 D2
Millhill La 30 D2
Moir Av 31 G2
Moir Cres 31 G2
Moir Dri 31 G2
Moir Pl 31 G2
Moir Ter 31 F2
Monktonhall Ter 30 B4
Mountjoy Ter 30 C1
Mucklets Av 30 A4
Mucklets Ct 30 A4
Mucklets Cres 30 B4
Mucklets Dri 30 A4
Mucklets Pl 30 A4
Musselburgh By-Pass 30 A5
New St 30 B2
Newbigging 30 D2
Newhailes Av 30 A2
Newhailes Cres 30 A2
Newhailes Rd 30 A2
North High St 30 B2
Old Craighall Rd 30 B5
Olive Bank Rd 30 A2
Park Av 31 E3
Park Ct 31 E3
Park Grove Pl 31 E3
Park Grove Ter 31 E3
Park La 31 E3
Park Vw 31 E3
Parsonage 30 D2
Pinkie Av 31 E3
Pinkie Hill Cres 31 E3
Pinkie Pl 31 E3
Pinkie Rd 30 D3
Pinkie Ter 31 E3
Promenade 30 B1
Ravenshaugh Cres 31 G2
Ravenshaugh Rd 31 F2
Riverside Gdns 30 B3
Rothesay Pl 30 D3
St Clements Gdns Nth 31 H4
St Clements Gdns Sth 31 H4
St Clements Ter 31 H4
St Michaels Av 30 C3
Salters Rd 31 F6
Short Hope St 30 C2
Smeaton Gro 30 D4
South St 30 C2
Station Rd 30 B3
Stoneybank Av 30 B4
Stoneybank Ct 30 B3
Stoneybank Cres 30 A3
Stoneybank Cres 30 B4
Stoneybank Dri 30 B3
Stoneybank Gdns 30 A3
Stoneybank Gdns Nth 30 B3
Stoneybank Gdns Sth 30 B3
Stoneybank Gro 30 B4
Stoneybank Pl 30 B4
Stoneybank Rd 30 B4
Stoneybank Ter 30 B4
Stoneyhill Av 30 A3
Stoneyhill Ct 30 A3
Stoneyhill Dri 30 A3
Stoneyhill Farm Rd 30 B3
Stoneyhill Gro 30 A3
Stoneyhill Pl 30 A3
Stoneyhill Rise 30 A3
Stoneyhill Road 30 A3
Stoneyhill Ter 30 A3
The Grove 31 E3
Watts Clo 30 B2
Wedderburn Ter 30 D4
Wemyss Gdns 31 H3
West Holmes Gdns 30 B2
Whitehill Av 30 A3
Whitehill Gdns 30 A4
Whitehill Rd 30 A4
Windsor Gdns 31 E2
Windsor Park 31 F2
Windsor Park Dri 31 F2
Windsor Park Ter 31 E2
Windy Wynd 30 D4
Woodside Gdns 31 E2

NEWTONGRANGE

Anderson Av 58 C2
Andrew Dodds Av 58 E1
Ash Gro 58 E1
Beechgrove Rd 58 E2
Beechwood Park 58 B2
Bevan Rd 58 E3
Blackcot Av 58 D3
Blackcot Dri 58 D3
Blackcot Pl 58 D3
Blackcot Rd 58 D3
Bogwood Ct 58 E1
Bogwood Rd 58 D1
Broadhurst Rd 58 D1
Bryans Av 58 B2
Bryans Rd 58 B2
Buckie Rd 58 E2
Burnside Cres 58 D1
Camp Rd 58 F2
Camp Wood Vw 58 E3
Cherry La 58 F2
Chester Vw 58 D3
Conifer Rd 58 E1
Cook Cres 58 E3
Coronation Pl 58 D1
Crawless Cres 58 E2
Dalhousie Rd 58 A2
Darcy Rd 58 E2
David Scott Av 58 E1
Dean Park 58 A3
Dean Park Pl 58 A3
Dougal Pl 58 E3
Easthouses Rd 58 D2
Eighth St 58 B3
Elm Pl 58 E2
Eskview Rd 58 D2
Ferguson Way 58 B4
Fifth St 58 B3
Finlay Pl 58 F2
First St 58 B4
Fourth St 58 B3
Galadale Abbey Gra 58 B2
Galadale Cres 58 B2
Galadale Dri 58 B2
Gardiner Pl 58 B2
Gordon St 58 D1
Hamilton Cres 58 C2
Hawthorn Cres 58 D1
Higginson Loan 58 F3
Hill Pl 58 E3
Holly Bank 58 E1
Hughes Cres 58 F2
Hursted Av 58 D1
John Humble St 58 E3
Kier Hardie Dri 58 E3
Kippielaw Park 58 D1
Laburnum Pl 58 E2
Langlaw Rd 58 E1
Larch Cres 58 F2
Laurel Bank Pl 58 E2
Laurel Bank Rd 58 E2
Lawfield Rd 58 E1
Leighton Cres 58 D1
Lilac Av 58 F2
Lime Gro 58 F2
Lingerwood Farm Cotts 58 C4
Lingerwood Rd 58 B4
Lothian Ter 58 B4
McCathie Dri 58 C2
McDiarmid Gro 58 B4
McKinnon Dri 58 F3
Main St 58 A3
Mansfield Av 58 B2
Mansfield Pl 58 B2
Mansfield Rd 58 B2
Mayfield Pl 58 E2
Mayfield Rd 58 D1
Monks Wood 58 B3
Monkswood Rd 58 B4
Morris Rd 58 C2
Murderdean Rd 58 A2
Myrtle Gro 58 E1
Newbattle Ind Est 58 C3
Newbattle Rd 58 A1
Ninth St 58 B3
Oak Cres 58 E2
Oak Pl 58 F2
Park Rd 58 B2
Pinewood Pl 58 E2
Pinewood Rd 58 E2
Pinewood View 58 E2
Poplar St 58 F2
Ramsay Cres 58 E3
Ramsay Walk 58 F3
Reed Dri 58 C2
Robert Smille Av 58 E3
Ross Pl 58 B2
Rowantree Rd 58 E2
Ruskin Pl 58 E3
St Annes Ct 58 B3
St Davids 58 B3
Saugh Cotts 58 B4
Second St 58 B4
Seventh St 58 B3
Sixth St 58 B3
Smithy Cotts 58 C4
Station Rd 58 A3
Steele Av 58 F2
Stevenson La 58 B4
Stobhill Rd 58 B4
Stone Av 58 E2
Stone Pl 58 D3
Suttieslea Cres 58 D2
Suttieslea Dri 58 C2
Suttieslea Pl 58 C2
Suttieslea Rd 58 C2
Suttieslea Walk 58 C2
Sycamore Rd 58 E2
Tenth St 58 B2
The Beeches 58 B1
The Square 58 B3
Third St 58 B3
Watt Gro 58 F3
Waverley Pk 58 D2
Waverley St 58 D3
Waverley Ter 58 D2
Westhouses Av 58 F3
Westhouses Dri 58 E3
Westhouses Rd 58 E3
Westhouses St 58 E3
Willow Rd 58 F2

PENICUIK

Alderbank 61 D8
Andrew Clo 61 C5
Ann St 61 C5
Armine Pl 61 F5
Arrass Gro 60 E4
Assynt Bank 61 E6
Avon Gro 61 E6
Baldwin Ct 61 C8
Balfour Ter 60 F3
Bank St 61 D7
Bavelaw Cres 61 B6
Beech Pl 61 D8
Bellmans Rd 61 C6
Belwood Cres 60 F3
Belwood Rd 60 C3
Blenheim Ct 60 E4
Bog Rd 61 C7
Boyd-Orr Dri 60 D4
Braidlaw Park 61 A7
Breck Ter 60 E4
Bridge St 61 D8
Brockwood Av 61 A6
Broomhill Av 61 C7
Broomhill Rd 61 C8
Brunstane Gdns 61 B6
Cairnbank Gdns 61 C8
Cairnbank Rd 61 C8
Caplan Way 61 A7
Carlops Av 61 C6
Carlops Cres 61 C6
Carlops Rd 61 A7
Carnethy Av 61 D6
Carnethy Ct 61 D6
Castlelaw Ct 61 D6
Catriona Ter 60 F3
Charles St 61 C5
Chisholm Ter 61 D5
Clerk Rd 61 B7
Corunna Ter 60 E4
Cowan Ter 61 D5
Craigfield Cres 61 C8
Cranston St 61 C7
Crockett Gdns 61 B7
Croft St 61 C8
Cruachan Ct 61 E6
Cuiken Av 61 C6
Cuiken Ter 61 B6
Cuikenburn 61 C5
Dean Pl 61 B6
Dean Rd 61 B6
Deanburn 61 B5
Dick Ter 61 D6
Dykes Rd 61 C5
East Queensway 61 D5
Eastfield 61 D6
Eastfield Dri 61 D6
Eastfield Farm Rd 61 D5
Eastfield Park Rd 61 D6
Edinburgh Rd 61 D6
Esk Bridge 61 E7
Eskhill 61 D6
Eskmill Rd 61 E7
Eskvale Cres 61 E6
Eskvale Dri 61 E6
Ewing St 61 D5
Fetteresk Cotts 61 C8
Fletcher Gro 60 D4
Friarton Gdns 61 A7
Gardners Walk 61 A6
Glaskill Ter 61 C6
Glen Pl 61 C6
Glencross Gdns 61 A7
Glenview 61 C6
Grahams Rd 60 F3
Greenhill Park 61 B6
Greenlaw Gro 60 E3
Grieve Ct 61 D5
Harkerburn Gdns 61 A6
Harpers Brae 61 F6
Hawkins Ter 60 F4
High St 61 D7
Imrie Pl 61 D7
INDUSTRIAL ESTATES:
Eastfield Ind Est 61 D6
Eskmill Ind Est 61 E7
Inkerman Ct 60 E4
Jackson St 61 C7
John Knox Pl 61 D7
John St 61 C6
Johnson 60 D4
Kirkhill Gdns 61 D7
Kirkhill Rd 61 D7
Kirklands 61 C7
Kirkton Bank 61 B7
Knightslaw Pl 61 B7
Laing Ter 61 D5
Lambs Pend 61 C7
Laverock Dri 61 B5
Lawers Sq 61 E5
Lawhead Pl 61 A6
Lawrie Dri 61 C5
Ledi Ter 61 E5
Livesay Ter 60 E4
Loanburn 61 C7
Loanburn Av 61 D6
Lomond Vale 61 E5
Lowrie Av 61 A7
Lyne Ter 61 E5
MacCormick Ter 60 D4

LIST OF PLACES OF INTEREST
TO CENTRE ENLARGEMENT

ESTATE PUBLICATIONS

STREET ATLASES

ASHFORD, TENTERDEN
BASILDON, BRENTWOOD
BASINGSTOKE, ANDOVER
BATH, BRADFORD ON AVON
BOURNEMOUTH, POOLE, CHRISTCHURCH
BRIGHTON, LEWES, NEWHAVEN, SEAFORD
BROMLEY (London Borough)
CHELMSFORD, BRAINTREE, MALDON, WITHAM
CHICHESTER, BOGNOR REGIS
COLCHESTER, CLACTON
CRAWLEY & MID SUSSEX
DERBY, HEANOR, CASTLE DONINGTON
EDINBURGH
EXETER, EXMOUTH
FAREHAM, GOSPORT
FOLKESTONE, DOVER, DEAL
GLOUCESTER, CHELTENHAM
GRAVESEND, DARTFORD
GUILDFORD, WOKING
HASTINGS, EASTBOURNE, HAILSHAM
HIGH WYCOMBE
I. OF WIGHT TOWNS
LEICESTER
MAIDSTONE
MANSFIELD
MEDWAY, GILLINGHAM
NEW FOREST TOWNS
NOTTINGHAM, EASTWOOD, HUCKNALL, ILKESTON
OXFORD
PLYMOUTH, IVYBRIDGE, SALTASH, TORPOINT
PORTSMOUTH, HAVANT
READING
REIGATE, BANSTEAD, LEATHERHEAD, DORKING
RYE & ROMNEY MARSH
ST. ALBANS, WELWYN, HATFIELD
SALISBURY, AMESBURY, WILTON
SEVENOAKS
SHREWSBURY
SLOUGH, MAIDENHEAD
SOUTHAMPTON, EASTLEIGH
SOUTHEND-ON-SEA
SWALE (Sittingbourne, Faversham, I. of Sheppey)
SWINDON, CHIPPENHAM, MARLBOROUGH
TAUNTON, BRIDGWATER
TELFORD
THANET, CANTERBURY, HERNE BAY, WHITSTABLE
TORBAY
TUNBRIDGE WELLS, TONBRIDGE, CROWBOROUGH
WATFORD, HEMEL HEMPSTEAD
WEALDEN TOWNS
WEYMOUTH
WINCHESTER, NEW ALRESFORD
WORTHING, LITTLEHAMPTON, ARUNDEL

LEISURE MAPS

SOUTH EAST (1:200,000)
KENT & EAST SUSSEX (1:150,000)
SURREY & SUSSEX (1:150,000)
SOUTHERN ENGLAND (1:200,000)
ISLE OF WIGHT (1:50,000)
WESSEX (1:200,000)
DEVON & CORNWALL (1:200,000)
CORNWELL (1:180,000)
DEVON (1:200,000)
DARTMOOR & SOUTH DEVON COAST (1:100,000)
EXMOOR & NORTH DEVON COAST (1:100,000)
GREATER LONDON (1:80,000)
A DAY OUT OF LONDON (1:425,000)
EAST ANGLIA (1:250,000)
THAMES & CHILTERNS (1:200,000)
COTSWOLDS & WYEDEAN (1:200,000)
HEART OF ENGLAND (1:250,000)
WALES (1:250,000)
THE SHIRES OF MIDDLE ENGLAND (1:250,000)
SHROPSHIRE, STAFFORDSHIRE (1:200,000)
PEAK DISTRICT (1:100,000)
SNOWDONIA (1:125,000)
YORKSHIRE & HUMBERSIDE (1:250,000)
YORKSHIRE DALES (1:250,000)
NORTH YORK MOORS (1:125,000)
NORTH WEST ENGLAND (1:200,000)
ISLE OF MAN (1:60,000)
NORTH PENNINES & LAKES (1:200,000)
LAKE DISTRICT (1:75,000)
BORDERS OF ENGLAND & SCOTLAND (1:200,000)
BURNS COUNTRY (1:200,000)
ISLE OF ARRAN (1:63,360)
ARGYLL & THE ISLES (1:200,000)
HEART OF SCOTLAND (1:200,000)
GREATER GLASGOW (1:150,000)
EDINBURGH (1:150,000)
FIFE (1:100,000)
LOCH LOMOND & TROSSACHS (1:150,000)
PERTHSHIRE (1:150,000)
FORT WILLIAM, BEN NEVIS, GLEN COE (1:185,000)
IONA (1:10,000) & MULL (1:115,000)
GRAMPIAN HIGHLANDS (1:185,000)
LOCH NESS & INVERNESS (1:150,000)
AVIEMORE & SPEY VALLEY (1:150,000)
SKYE & LOCHALSH (1:130,000)
CAITHNESS & SUTHERLAND (1:185,000)
WESTERN ISLES (1:125,000)
ORKNEY & SHETLAND (1:128,000)
ENGLAND & WALES (1:650,000)
SCOTLAND (1:500,000)
HISTORIC SCOTLAND (1:500,000)
SCOTLAND CLAN MAP (1:625,000)
GREAT BRITAIN (1:1,100,000)

COUNTY ATLASES

AVON
AVON & SOMERSET
BERKSHIRE
CHESHIRE
CORNWALL
DEVON
DORSET
ESSEX
HAMPSHIRE
HAMPSHIRE (Large Format)
HERTFORDSHIRE
KENT (64pp)
KENT (128pp)
OXFORDSHIRE
SHROPSHIRE
SOMERSET
SURREY
SUSSEX (64pp)
SUSSEX (128pp)
WILTSHIRE

EUROPEAN LEISURE MAPS

EUROPE (1:3,100,000)
BENELUX (1:600,000)
FRANCE (1:1,000,000)
GERMANY (1:1,000,000)
GREECE & THE AEGEAN (1:1,000,000)
IRELAND (1:625,000)
ITALY (1:1,000,000)
MEDITERRANEAN CRUISING (1:5,000,000)
SCANDINAVIA (1:2,600,000)
SPAIN & PORTUGAL (1:1,000,000)
THE ALPS (1:1,000,000)
WORLD (1:35,000,000)
WORLD FLAT
WORLD FLAT WITH FLAGS

ESTATE PUBLICATIONS are also
sole distributors in the U.K. for:
ORDNANCE SURVEY, Republic of Ireland
ORDNANCE SURVEY, Northern Ireland

ROAD ATLAS

MOTORING IN THE SOUTH
(1:200,000)

STREET PLANS

BARNSTAPLE & ILFRACOMBE
BODMIN & WADEBRIDGE
NEWQUAY
NEWTOWN & WELSHPOOL
PENZANCE & ST IVES
ST ALBANS
TRURO
WESTON-SUPER-MARE

Catalogue and prices from ESTATE PUBLICATIONS,
Bridewell House, Tenterden, Kent TN30 6JB.
Tel: 05806 4225   Fax: 05806 3720